Summer Favourites

Summer Favourites

Essential, delicious recipes
from the bestselling
VJ Cooks

VANYA INSULL

ALLEN&UNWIN
SYDNEY · MELBOURNE · AUCKLAND · LONDON

For all of my amazing and
supportive family and friends

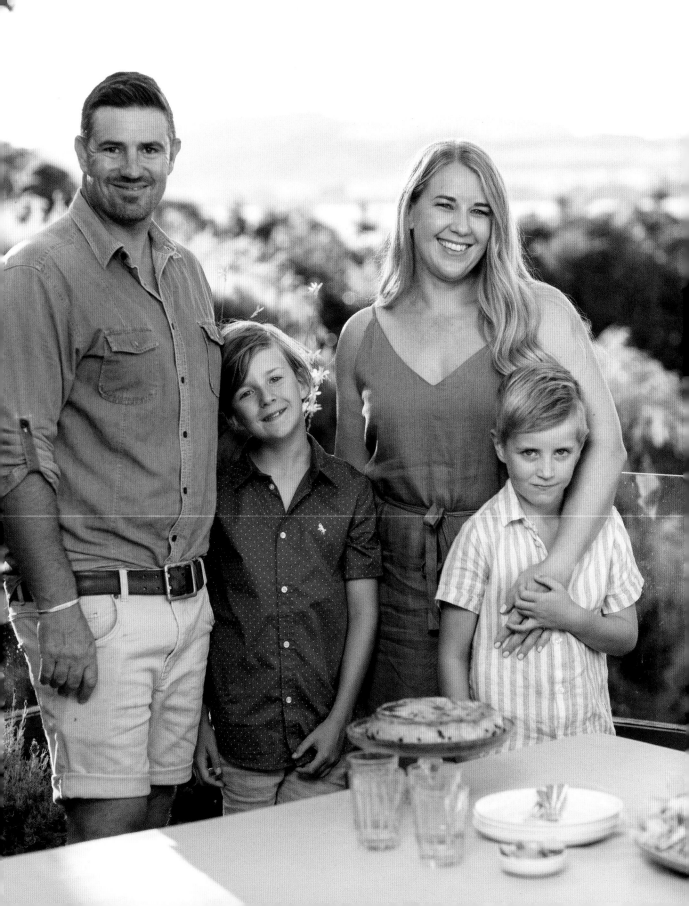

Contents

Introduction 9
About My Recipes 12

Summer Classics 15
Everyday Dinners 45
Salads to Impress 93
Home Baking 119
Desserts 159

Acknowledgements 201
Index 203

Introduction

**Wow! I can't believe we are on to cookbook two! And, just quietly,
I think this one could be even better than *Everyday Favourites*.**

A big thanks to all of you who went out and bought my first cookbook. It was so exciting to see it in real life, on the shelves in bookstores and being sold around New Zealand and the world. I have loved seeing all the photos from readers showing pages of their copy splattered with food, and reading the comments from people saying how much they enjoyed the recipes.

I remember the week after *Everyday Favourites* was released. Michelle Hurley, my publisher from Allen & Unwin, called me and said, 'Well, we better start thinking about cookbook number two.'

'Can't we just enjoy this one first?' I replied with a smile. She laughed and pointed out that, based on the popularity of *Everyday Favourites* after just one week, a second book should definitely be on the horizon. And now, here it is! I'm hoping you'll love this one just as much as the first.

With summer coming up, I thought it was the perfect time to share my favourite light and fresh recipes. You'll see that the book has five chapters. The first is 'Summer Classics', which features lots of my delicious entertaining and barbecue recipes. The second chapter, 'Everyday Dinners', has more of my easy, go-to recipes for busy weeknights. I know that recipes like this are what people love most about my website vjcooks.com.

It wouldn't be a summer cookbook without a chapter on salads. 'Salads to Impress' has my latest picks — most of them are platter-style salads that are simple to put together and perfect for feeding a crowd.

And then to the sweet stuff. In the 'Home Baking' chapter I have shared more of my favourite loaves, slices and biscuits. I'm also happy to say that there is a 'Desserts' chapter, featuring some of the biggest hits from my website and social media — Brownie Trifle and Mini Pavlova Wreath — as well as newbies like my Baked Lemon and Passionfruit Cheesecake (which appears on the front cover).

The 'Kids Fave' stickers have been used again to help you identify the most family-friendly meals and baking.

I have had the best time putting this cookbook together, and I really hope you find inspiration in these pages and new favourites to enjoy this summer and beyond. Whether you're entertaining with friends and family or looking for a quick and tasty midweek meal, it's all in here.

It has been so amazing to receive the incredible feedback from *Everyday Favourites*. Nothing beats walking into a bookstore with my sons and seeing their proud faces when they spot it on the shelves. And now I get to do it all again with this book, so thank you for buying it. Make sure you share your creations with me — seeing how much you enjoy the recipes is why I do what I do.

Happy cooking,

VJ x

About My Recipes

For those who are new to my recipes . . . I'm a busy mum, so I design my recipes to take the stress out of feeding a family. I try to keep them as simple as possible, using everyday ingredients that you probably already have in the pantry or fridge — and that kids are likely to be happy to eat.

Most of my dinner recipes are super-versatile, and I've provided tips on alternative ingredients as well as serving suggestions. Feel free to add or swap in any appropriate vegetables that you have hiding in the back of your fridge. Similarly, some of the baking and dessert recipes in this book call for fresh fruit, but if the fruits listed aren't readily available locally you can usually substitute them with others — or even use canned fruit.

While most of my dinner recipes feed a family of four, a few of them make a larger quantity because I like to freeze extra portions for another meal at a later date. Once the leftovers have cooled to room temperature, I transfer them to an airtight container or sealable bag and freeze them for up to 3 months. When I need a meal in a hurry, I defrost them and reheat until piping hot.

I also love to freeze baking to have on hand for a quick lunchbox filler. Cookie dough, baked muffins and loaves all freeze well, so I often double the recipes and freeze half.

I use fan bake for the majority of my cooking, unless stated otherwise. If you are using a conventional oven instead, the general rule of thumb is to add 20°C (70°F), so for example 180°C (350°F) fan bake would be 200°C (400°F) in a conventional oven. All ovens have their own quirks. You probably already know if yours runs hot or cold, so feel free to adjust the cook times and temperatures accordingly.

When baking, I always line my tins and trays with baking paper. This prevents my baking from sticking to the tin and ensures everything comes out in one piece. It also makes for an easy clean-up.

I specify the size of my baking tins in my recipes, but if your tins are slightly different the recipes will still work! If your tin is larger the bake time will be shorter, whereas if it's smaller it may take longer for your baking to fully cook through. Just keep an eye on the time, and bake until a skewer inserted into your baking comes out clean.

Master Measurements

I use New Zealand standard measures in my recipes:

1 teaspoon = 5 ml (⅙ fl oz)
1 tablespoon = 15 ml (½ fl oz)
¼ cup of liquid = 60 ml (2 fl oz)
½ cup of liquid = 125 ml (4 fl oz)
1 cup of liquid = 250 ml (9 fl oz)

The weight of a cup of dry ingredients will vary depending on the mass of the ingredients. These are some of the common quantities I use in my baking and this cookbook:

1 cup of plain flour = 150 g (5½ oz)
1 cup of white or caster sugar = 220 g (7¾ oz)
1 cup of brown sugar (firmly packed) = 200 g (7 oz)
1 cup of icing sugar = 130 g (4½ oz)
1 cup of cocoa powder = 90 g (3¼ oz)
1 cup of grated cheese = 100 g (3½ oz)
1 Weet-Bix = 17 g (½ oz)

Summer Classics

What's in this Chapter

**Barbecued Fish Tacos with
Pineapple Salsa** p18

**Roasted Pumpkin
and Feta Tart** p20

**Barbecued Satay
Chicken Skewers** p22

**Smashed Potatoes with
Herby Chipotle Sauce** p24

**Creamy Spinach
Cob Loaf** p26

**Breakfast Pizza
Slab** p30

**Barbecued Lamb
Kofta Platter** p32

**XL Brie and Cranberry
Wreath** p34

**Herby Chicken
Dippers** p36

**Chicken and Zucchini
Pesto Pasta** p38

**Barbecued Lamb Steaks
with Home-made
Chimichurri** p40

**Crispy Tuna
Cakes** p42

Barbecued Fish Tacos with Pineapple Salsa

One of my favourite things about summer is eating fresh fish!
Snapper, gurnard or tarakihi would be perfect in these fish tacos.
The zesty Pineapple Salsa gives them a real tropical hit.

Pineapple Salsa

½ fresh pineapple, finely
   diced
100 g (3½ oz) cherry
   tomatoes, finely diced
2 spring onions, finely sliced
½ fresh red chilli, finely
   chopped
juice of ½ lime
1 handful fresh coriander,
   finely chopped

500 g (1 lb 2 oz) firm white
   fish fillets
2 Tbsp olive oil
1 Tbsp Cajun seasoning
salt and cracked black
   pepper, to season
8 small tortillas
¼ iceberg lettuce, shredded
flesh of 1 avocado, sliced
125 g (4½ oz) sour cream
fresh coriander, to serve
lime wedges, to serve

1. To make the Pineapple Salsa, combine the ingredients in a bowl. Cover and chill until needed.

2. Slice the fish fillets into thin strips. Whisk the oil, Cajun seasoning and the salt and pepper in a bowl. Add the fish and turn to coat.

3. Grill the fish on a hot barbecue for a couple of minutes on each side, until cooked through.

4. Just before serving, toast the tortillas on the barbecue for about 1 minute on each side.

5. Fill the tortillas with the grilled fish, lettuce, avocado and sour cream, and top with Pineapple Salsa, coriander and a squeeze of lime juice.

Roasted Pumpkin and Feta Tart

It's the caramelised onions that make this vegetarian tart special. Topped with roasted pumpkin, feta and rosemary, it makes a delicious starter or lunch, or can be served with a green salad as a main course.

1 kg (2 lb 4 oz) pumpkin, peeled and cubed
2 Tbsp maple syrup
4 Tbsp olive oil
salt and cracked black pepper, to season
4 onions, sliced
½ tsp salt
2 Tbsp brown sugar
2 Tbsp balsamic vinegar
2 sheets puff pastry
100 g (3½ oz) feta or goat cheese, crumbled
2 Tbsp chopped fresh rosemary
1 egg, whisked

Tips and tricks

* *The onions take a long time to cook. Don't be tempted to increase the heat to speed up this process as they will burn.*

1. Preheat the oven to 200°C (400°F) fan bake. Line a baking tray with baking paper.

2. Arrange the pumpkin in a single layer on the prepared tray. Combine the maple syrup with 2 tablespoons of the oil and the salt and pepper. Drizzle the syrup over the pumpkin, then cook for 45 minutes, until soft.

3. Heat the remaining 2 tablespoons of oil in a large frying pan over a low heat. Add the onions and ½ tsp salt and cook gently for 20 minutes, stirring occasionally.

4. When the onions are soft, add the sugar and vinegar and continue to cook over a low heat for 15 minutes, until caramelised.

5. Reduce the oven to 180°C (350°F) fan bake. Line a baking tray with baking paper.

6. Place the pastry sheets on the tray, overlapping slightly, then press down on the join to seal.

7. Spread the caramelised onions over the pastry, leaving a gap of about 5 cm (2 in) around the edge. Arrange the cooked pumpkin on top then sprinkle with the feta or goat cheese and rosemary.

8. Fold the pastry edges back onto the tart, pinching the corners together. Brush with the whisked egg.

9. Bake for 45 minutes until the pastry is golden and cooked through. Allow to cool slightly before serving.

Barbecued Satay Chicken Skewers

I love the flavour of barbecued chicken. The best thing about this recipe is you turn the extra marinade into a tasty dipping sauce.

500 g (1 lb 2 oz) boneless
  chicken thighs
½ cup coconut cream
1 Tbsp lime juice
fresh coriander or parsley, to
  serve
lime wedges, to serve

Satay Marinade
½ cup crunchy peanut butter
½ cup boiling water
¼ cup low-salt soy sauce
¼ cup sweet chilli sauce
1 Tbsp brown sugar
2 tsp crushed ginger

1. Cut each chicken thigh into 3 even strips. Divide between 8 skewers. Place in a large dish or container.

2. To make the Satay Marinade, mix the ingredients together in a small pot.

3. Pour ¼ cup Satay Marinade over the chicken skewers and turn to coat. Cover and marinate in the fridge for at least 30 minutes.

4. Grill the chicken skewers on a barbecue for 15–20 minutes, until cooked through.

5. While the chicken is cooking, gently warm the remaining Satay Marinade over a medium heat.

6. Add the coconut cream and bring to the boil. Reduce the heat to a simmer and cook, stirring, for 10 minutes. Remove from the heat and stir in the lime juice.

7. Serve drizzled with satay sauce and garnished with coriander and lime wedges.

Tips and tricks

• *If you have time you could prepare the chicken and marinade the night before and store, covered, in the fridge until needed.*

• *If using bamboo skewers, soak them in cold water for half an hour before using. This prevents them from burning while cooking.*

• *Smooth peanut butter will also work for the satay sauce.*

• *This recipe can be easily doubled to serve more people.*

KIDS'
FAVE

Smashed Potatoes with Herby Chipotle Sauce

These smashed potatoes turn out super-crispy on the outside and soft on the inside. I serve them topped with a punchy, herby chipotle sauce.

1 kg (2 lb 4 oz) baby potatoes
1 tsp salt
2 Tbsp olive oil
1 tsp sea salt
fresh herbs, to serve

Herby Chipotle Sauce
¼ cup mayonnaise
1 Tbsp chipotle sauce
1 Tbsp milk
1 tsp lemon juice
1 clove garlic, finely crushed
1 handful fresh basil, roughly
  chopped
1 handful fresh parsley,
  roughly chopped
salt and cracked black
  pepper, to taste

1. Preheat the oven to 210°C (410°F) fan bake.

2. Place the potatoes and salt in a large pot, cover with boiling water and gently simmer over a medium heat for 15 minutes, until tender when pierced with a fork.

3. Pour the oil into a baking tray and place in the oven to heat for 5 minutes.

4. Drain the potatoes. Place the lid back on the pot and shake the pot to break up the potatoes a bit. Remove the heated baking tray from the oven and gently pour the potatoes into the tray, turning them to coat in the warm oil. Smash each potato down using a spatula.

5. Sprinkle with sea salt and bake for 25 minutes, until the potatoes are golden and cooked through.

6. While the potatoes are cooking, make the Herby Chipotle Sauce by blending the ingredients with a stick blender until smooth and combined.

7. Serve the crispy potatoes drizzled with Herby Chipotle Sauce and garnished with fresh herbs.

Creamy Spinach Cob Loaf

This cob loaf is one of the most popular savoury recipes on my website. I cut the top and inner part of the loaf into strips and bake them into crouton dippers. Fresh vegetable sticks also work well (I use cucumber, carrots, celery and and capsicum), as do crackers.

250 g (9 oz) frozen spinach

1 cob loaf

125 g (4½ oz) sour cream

250 g (9 oz) cream cheese

35 g (1¼ oz) packet onion soup

100 g (3½ oz) grated mozzarella

½ cup milk

vegetable sticks, to serve (optional)

1. Preheat the oven to 170°C (325°F) fan bake. Line a baking tray with baking paper.

2. Place the spinach in a microwave-proof bowl and microwave for 1 minute. Transfer it to a sieve and squeeze out the excess water.

3. Cut the top off the cob loaf and gently remove the inner part of the loaf. Cut into 2 cm (¾ in) strips, then place on the prepared tray with the cob loaf.

4. Bake for 10 minutes while you make the dip.

5. Place the spinach in a pot and cook over a low heat for 1 minute.

6. Add the sour cream and cream cheese and cook, stirring, until the cream cheese has melted and everything is combined.

7. Stir in the onion soup, then add the mozzarella. Add the milk and stir to combine.

8. Pour the hot dip into the hollowed-out cob loaf and serve with the crouton strips and vegetable sticks (if using) on the side.

Breakfast Pizza Slab

I was inspired to make this dish a few years ago after ordering a slice of breakfast pizza from the former Art Deco Café in Esk Valley, Hawke's Bay. Once I got home I knew I had to make a version of my own.

Pizza Dough

1 cup warm water
1 tsp sugar
1 tsp active dry yeast
2½ cups plain flour
2 Tbsp olive oil
1 tsp salt

½ cup tomato relish or
  chutney
250 g (9 oz) streaky bacon
8 eggs
½ cup grated mozzarella
¼ cup finely grated parmesan
salt and cracked black
  pepper, to taste
fresh Italian parsley, to serve

Tips and tricks

- *You can use leftover Christmas ham instead of the bacon.*

- *Great additions would be thinly sliced tomatoes, caramelised onions or a garnish of chives.*

- *This pizza can be eaten cold the next day, so it's a great option for a picnic.*

1. To make the Pizza Dough, place the warm water and sugar in a large bowl or the bowl of a stand mixer and stir to dissolve. Add the yeast and stir again. Cover with a clean tea towel and set aside for 10 minutes.

2. Add the flour, oil and salt and mix to combine. Knead by hand or on low with the dough hook for 5 minutes until smooth and a little sticky.

3. Cover with a clean tea towel and allow to rise in a warm place for at least 30 minutes, until doubled in size.

4. Grease a 38 x 25 cm (15 x 10 in) baking tray.

5. Turn out the Pizza Dough onto a well-floured surface and roll out into a rectangle big enough to fit the prepared tray. Transfer it to the tray and push it into the corners to fit. Allow to rise for 20 minutes.

6. While the dough rises, preheat the oven to 220°C (425°F) fan bake.

7. When ready to cook, spread the relish over the risen dough and arrange the bacon on top. Carefully crack the eggs into the gaps. Top with the mozzarella and parmesan. Season well with salt and pepper.

8. Bake for 20 minutes until the top is golden and the base is cooked through.

9. Scatter with parsley and cut into 8 large pieces to serve.

Barbecued Lamb Kofta Platter

This is a great recipe to prepare in advance. Make the lamb koftas, thread them onto skewers and have them in the fridge ready to barbecue at dinnertime. I like to serve them on a large platter with all the fillings alongside, so everyone can help themselves.

Lamb Koftas

500 g (1 lb 2 oz) lamb mince
¼ cup breadcrumbs
½ red onion, grated
1 tsp dried mixed herbs
1 tsp ground coriander
1 tsp ground cumin
1 tsp cinnamon
1 tsp salt
¼ tsp ground white pepper

To serve

4 large flatbreads or wraps
1 cup hummus
100 g (3½ oz) cherry
  tomatoes, halved
30 g (1 oz) rocket leaves or
  mesclun
50 g (1¾ oz) feta
1 handful fresh mint, torn

1. To make the Lamb Koftas, combine the ingredients in a large bowl.

2. With damp hands, divide the mixture into 8 equal portions and shape onto 8 skewers.

3. Grill the koftas on the barbecue for 15 minutes, turning every few minutes, until nicely browned and cooked through.

4. Just before serving, warm the flatbreads on the barbecue for about 30 seconds each.

5. To serve, layer up your toasted flatbreads with hummus, a kofta or two, cherry tomatoes and rocket or mesclun. Sprinkle with the feta and mint.

Tips and tricks

- *If using bamboo skewers, soak them in cold water while you prepare the koftas. This prevents them from burning while cooking.*

- *These koftas can be served individually or on a large platter.*

- *Feel free to add your favourite salad ingredients and sauces.*

XL Brie and Cranberry Wreath

If you're looking for the ultimate dinner party or Christmas showstopper, look no further! You can usually find extra-large rounds of brie over the festive season, but if you can't get your hands on one then you can use 3 smaller brie rounds instead.

900 g (2 lb) brie round
8 par-baked buffet rolls
100 g (3½ oz) cranberry
  sauce
3 Tbsp garlic butter, softened
1 Tbsp runny honey
fresh rosemary and thyme
  sprigs, to serve
extra buffet rolls, to serve

1. Preheat the oven to 180°C (350°F) fan bake. Line a baking tray with baking paper.

2. Place the brie in the centre of the prepared tray.

3. Cut the rolls in half vertically and horizontally so you have 4 quarters. Spread the cranberry sauce on one side of each piece.

4. Arrange the roll pieces around the brie. Brush with the garlic butter.

5. Bake for 15 minutes, until the rolls are golden and the brie has melted in the centre.

6. Drizzle with the honey and garnish with thyme and rosemary sprigs.

7. Serve hot, with extra rolls on the side.

Herby Chicken Dippers

You won't believe how much flavour is packed into these chicken dippers. It's the perfect recipe to make in summer when zucchini is in season. Serve with a fresh green salad for dinner or make smaller dippers to share as nibbles at a party or barbecue.

2 medium zucchini
500 g (1 lb 2 oz) chicken mince
½ cup breadcrumbs
1 egg
2 spring onions, finely chopped
2 cloves garlic, crushed
2 Tbsp finely chopped fresh mint, plus extra for garnish
2 Tbsp finely chopped fresh parsley
1 tsp ground cumin
1 tsp salt
¼ tsp cracked black pepper

Minty Dipping Sauce
¾ cup Greek yoghurt
1 handful fresh mint, finely chopped
1 tsp finely grated lemon zest
1 Tbsp lemon juice
¼ tsp salt

1. Coarsely grate the zucchini onto a clean tea towel. Pull up the edges and wring out as much liquid as possible.

2. Transfer to a large mixing bowl. Add all the remaining ingredients and mix until combined.

3. Roll the mixture into about 24 balls about the size of golf balls. Place on a plate, flatten slightly with the palm of your hand and chill for 10 minutes to firm up.

4. To make the Minty Dipping Sauce, combine the ingredients in a bowl and chill until needed.

5. Cook the chicken dippers on a hot barbecue for 15–20 minutes until nicely browned and cooked through.

6. Serve with the Minty Dipping Sauce on the side, and garnish with extra mint if desired.

Tips and tricks
- *This mixture could also be made into chicken burger patties.*
- *To save time I use a pull chopper to finely chop my herbs and spring onion together.*

KIDS' FAVE

Chicken and Zucchini Pesto Pasta

This is a great recipe to throw together when you want to use up leftover chicken. For a vegetarian version, just leave out the chicken.

300 g (10½ oz) bow-tie pasta

2 tsp olive oil

3 zucchini, sliced

3 cloves garlic, crushed

½ tsp chilli flakes (optional)

250 g (9 oz) cooked chicken, chopped

180 g (6 oz) cherry tomatoes, halved

150 g (5½ oz) pesto

salt and cracked black pepper, to taste

1 handful fresh basil, chopped

2 Tbsp grated parmesan, to serve

1. Cook the pasta according to the packet instructions until al dente. Drain, reserving 1 cup of the pasta cooking water.

2. Heat the oil in a large frying pan over a medium heat. Add the zucchini and cook for a few minutes on each side until starting to brown. Stir in the garlic and chilli (if using).

3. Add the chicken and cherry tomatoes to the pan. Once the chicken is heated through, add the pesto and reserved pasta water. Stir to combine, simmer for 2 minutes then season to taste with salt and pepper.

4. Add the cooked pasta and stir to coat in the sauce. Stir in most of the basil, reserving a little for garnish.

5. Serve immediately, topped with the parmesan and remaining basil.

Tips and tricks

- *If you don't have leftover cooked chicken, cut a chicken breast in half horizontally, season well and pan-fry for 5 minutes on each side until cooked through.*

- *Toasted pine nuts also make a great addition.*

Barbecued Lamb Steaks with Home-made Chimichurri

The trick to getting a great tasting chimichurri is to let it marinate in the fridge so all those intense flavours come together to make the best sauce, perfect served over thinly sliced barbecued lamb.

500 g (1 lb 2 oz) lamb steaks
2 Tbsp olive oil
2 tsp ground cumin
salt and cracked black
  pepper, to season

Chimichurri

¼ cup olive oil
2 tsp red wine vinegar
1 clove garlic, crushed
2 handfuls fresh Italian
  parsley, finely chopped
¼ tsp chilli flakes
¼ tsp salt

1. To marinate the lamb steaks, place them in a dish or container with the oil and cumin, and season well with salt and pepper. Turn to coat, then cover and chill for 2 hours.

2. To make the Chimichurri, combine the ingredients in a small jug. Chill for 2 hours.

3. Grill the lamb on a hot barbecue for a few minutes on each side, until cooked to your liking. Cover and allow to rest for 10 minutes.

4. Carve into strips and arrange on a platter. Pour the Chimichurri down the centre of the lamb slices and serve immediately.

Tips and tricks

- *This Chimichurri sauce is also great served with barbecued chicken thighs or beef steaks.*

- *Extra Chimichurri can be stored in a jar in the fridge for up to a week.*

Crispy Tuna Cakes

These delicious fish cakes are a great way to make pantry staples go a long way. The panko crumbs make them nice and crispy, perfect served with home-made lemon aioli and a side salad.

Lemon Aioli
¼ cup mayonnaise
½ clove garlic, crushed
1 tsp finely grated lemon zest
2 tsp lemon juice
salt and cracked black
   pepper, to taste

180 g (6 oz) canned tuna
2 cups mashed potato
1 cup plain flour
1 spring onion, finely sliced
1 egg
1 Tbsp mayonnaise
1 tsp finely grated lemon zest
salt and cracked black
   pepper, to season
1 cup panko crumbs
olive oil, for frying
chives, to serve
lemon wedges, to serve

1. To make the Lemon Aioli, mix the ingredients in a small bowl and chill until needed.

2. Combine the tuna, mashed potato, flour, spring onion, egg, mayonnaise and lemon zest in a large bowl, and season with salt and pepper. Stir well to combine.

3. Using an ice cream scoop or large spoon, scoop up the mixture and shape into about 16 balls with your hands. Roll each ball in panko crumbs, then press it down to create a patty shape.

4. Heat a few tablespoons of oil in a large non-stick frying pan over a medium heat.

5. Working in batches, fry the patties for a few minutes on each side until golden and cooked through. Keep them warm in a low oven while you fry the rest, adding more oil between batches as needed.

6. Serve the hot tuna cakes with the Lemon Aioli, chives and lemon wedges.

Tips and tricks

- *These make great party nibbles. Just make them about half the size and keep them in a warm oven until you're ready to serve them with the dipping sauce.*

- *If you don't have panko crumbs you can use dried breadcrumbs instead.*

- *The patties can be made in advance, then covered and chilled until needed.*

KIDS'
FAVE

Everyday
Dinners

What's in this Chapter

One-pot Meatballs and Gnocchi p48

Chicken, Corn and Spinach Filo Pie p50

Beer-battered Fish Burgers p52

Sticky Pineapple Chicken Bowls p54

Classic Chicken Korma p56

Barbecued Steak Fajitas p58

Quick Smoked Salmon Pasta with Capers p62

Meatball Subs p64

Sweet and Sour Pork p66

**Southern-style
Fried Chicken** p68

**Vegetarian
Lasagne** p70

**Korean Beef
on Rice** p74

**Chicken Parmigiana
Tray Bake** p76

**Pork Lettuce
Cups** p80

**Pumpkin, Haloumi and
Cauliflower Curry** p82

**Beef and Noodle
Stir-fry** p84

**Moroccan Lamb
Pies** p86

**One-pot Chicken
and Lemon Orzo** p88

One-pot Meatballs and Gnocchi

I had to include this recipe here, as it's such a fan favourite. The gnocchi cooks in the sauce so there is no need to pre-cook it. If you want to make your meatballs from scratch, use the Meatball Subs recipe on page 64. Serve with a salad and crusty garlic bread.

1 Tbsp olive oil
400 g (14 oz) meatballs
  (store-bought, or see
  page 64)
2 cloves garlic, crushed
500 g (1 lb 2 oz) gnocchi
1 cup vegetable stock
1 Tbsp honey
1 Tbsp dried Italian herbs
400 g (14 oz) can crushed
  tomatoes
100 g (3½ oz) mozzarella,
  sliced
fresh basil or parsley,
  to serve

1. Heat the oil in a large pan over a medium heat. Add the meatballs and cook for about 5 minutes, until nicely browned.

2. Stir in the garlic, then the gnocchi.

3. Mix together the stock, honey and Italian herbs. Add to the pan along with the crushed tomatoes and mix gently to combine. Simmer for 10 minutes, until the meatballs and gnocchi are cooked through.

4. Arrange the mozzarella slices on top of the meatballs and gnocchi, cover and cook until melted.

5. Sprinkle with fresh herbs and serve immediately.

Tips and tricks

- *Feel free to use your favourite meatballs — pork, lamb or beef would all work well.*

- *I use vacuum-sealed packets of gnocchi, which can be found in the pasta section of the supermarket.*

KIDS' FAVE

Chicken, Corn and Spinach Filo Pie

This delicious pie is based on my popular mini chicken and sweetcorn pies. To give it a summer feel I have topped it with crunchy filo pastry and upped the veg factor with the addition of frozen spinach.

1 Tbsp olive oil
1 onion, finely sliced
3 cloves garlic, crushed
500 g (1 lb 2 oz) boneless
   chicken thighs, diced
250 g (9 oz) frozen spinach
2 cups frozen corn, thawed
1¼ cups cream
2 tsp dried mixed herbs
2 Tbsp water
1 Tbsp cornflour
salt and cracked black
   pepper, to taste
6 sheets filo pastry
2 Tbsp butter, melted
1 tsp sesame seeds

1. Preheat the oven to 190°C (375°F) fan bake.

2. Heat the oil in a large ovenproof frying pan or casserole dish over a medium heat. Sauté the onion for a few minutes until soft, then stir in the garlic.

3. Add the chicken and cook, stirring, until nicely browned.

4. Place the spinach in a microwave-proof bowl and microwave for 2 minutes. Transfer it to a sieve and squeeze out the excess water.

5. Add the spinach, corn, cream and mixed herbs to the pan and stir to combine.

6. Mix the water and cornflour in a small bowl. Add to the frying pan and cook, stirring, until the filling thickens up. Season with salt and pepper, then remove from the heat.

7. Brush a sheet of filo with butter, scrunch softly and place on top of the pie filling. Repeat with the remaining filo until the filling is completely covered.

8. Sprinkle with the sesame seeds and bake for 25 minutes, until the filo is golden and crispy. Serve immediately.

Tips and tricks
- *If you don't have an ovenproof frying pan or casserole dish, transfer the cooked chicken mixture to an oven dish before topping with filo.*

- *Swap the filo for puff pastry if you prefer.*

Beer-battered Fish Burgers

Beer batter is a great way to get a light and crunchy coating on your fish. You can serve it as burgers like this or it is just as good served on its own with home-made chips.

Beer Batter

1 cup self-raising flour
1 egg, whisked
1 tsp salt
330 ml (11¼ fl oz) beer

1 litre (35 fl oz) oil, for deep-frying
2 Tbsp plain flour
400 g (14 oz) firm white fish fillets

To serve

4 burger buns
4 Tbsp tartare sauce
4 lemon wedges
¼ iceberg lettuce, shredded

1. To make the Beer Batter, place the self-raising flour, egg and salt in a large mixing bowl. Add the beer and whisk to combine.

2. To cook the fish, heat the oil in a large cast-iron dish over a medium-high heat.

3. Place the plain flour on a plate. Coat a fish fillet in the plain flour, then the Beer Batter. Allow the excess batter to drip off, then place the fish in the hot oil.

4. Cook 2 pieces of fish at a time for a few minutes on each side, until the batter is golden and crispy and the fish is cooked through. Transfer to a paper towel. Repeat with the remaining fish, reducing the heat if the oil gets too hot.

5. To assemble the burgers, warm the buns then spread them with tartare sauce. Divide the fish pieces between the bun bases and drizzle with juice from the lemon wedges. Finish with the lettuce and bun tops and serve immediately.

Tips and tricks

- *Make sure you use oil with a high smoke point, such as rice bran or canola oil, for deep-frying. Keep an eye on it so it doesn't get too hot, and turn it down between batches if necessary.*

Sticky Pineapple Chicken Bowls

These bowls are so fresh and delicious. The combination of the sticky chicken and rice with avocado, radish and edamame beans is a family favourite.

1 tsp sesame oil
600 g (1 lb 5 oz) boneless
 chicken thighs, diced
400g (14 oz) can pineapple
 pieces
3 Tbsp low-salt soy sauce
2 Tbsp sweet chilli sauce
1 Tbsp cornflour
1 tsp crushed garlic
1 tsp crushed ginger

To serve

2 cups cooked rice
1 cup edamame beans,
 cooked
2 radishes, finely sliced
flesh of 1 avocado, sliced
1 spring onion, finely sliced
1 tsp sesame seeds

1. Heat the sesame oil in a non-stick frying pan. Add the chicken and cook, stirring, for 5 minutes.

2. Drain the can of pineapple pieces, reserving the juice. Add 1 cup of pineapple pieces to the frying pan with the chicken and cook for 3 minutes, until the pineapple starts to brown.

3. To make the sauce, measure 100 ml (3½ fl oz) of the reserved pineapple juice into a bowl or jug. Whisk in the soy sauce, sweet chilli sauce, cornflour, garlic and ginger.

4. Make a gap in the centre of the frying pan, add the sauce and cook, stirring, until the sauce thickens up and the chicken is cooked through.

5. To serve, divide the cooked rice between 4 serving bowls, then top with the sticky chicken and pineapple. Add some edamame beans and some sliced radish, avocado and spring onion to each bowl and sprinkle with sesame seeds.

Tips and tricks

- *Diced pork would also be amazing in this dish.*

- *Leave out the radishes if you don't like them!*

- *I like to give the leftover pineapple pieces to my kids as a snack or save them to use on a pizza.*

KIDS'
FAVE

Classic Chicken Korma

The chicken in this curry turns out so tender and is packed full of flavour.
The yoghurt marinade and ground almonds make all the difference.

½ cup natural yoghurt

2 Tbsp tomato paste

2 cloves garlic, crushed

2 tsp crushed ginger

500g (1 lb 2 oz) chicken
 thighs, diced

1 Tbsp butter

1 onion, finely sliced

1 tsp ground cumin

1 tsp ground turmeric

1 tsp garam masala

½ cup cream

½ cup chicken stock

¼ cup ground almonds

1 tsp sugar

fresh coriander, to serve

To serve

2 cups cooked rice

4 small roti, toasted

1. Combine the yoghurt, tomato paste, garlic and ginger in a medium bowl. Add the chicken and stir to coat. Marinate in the fridge for at least 30 minutes.

2. Melt the butter in a large frying pan over a medium heat. Add onion and sauté for 5 minutes.

3. Add the cumin, turmeric and garam masala and fry off for a few minutes.

4. Add the marinated chicken and cook for 5 minutes.

5. Stir in the cream, stock, ground almonds and sugar, then simmer for 10–15 minutes, until the chicken is cooked through.

6. Serve garnished with coriander and accompanied by rice and roti.

Tips and tricks

- *This is a great recipe to double, because you can freeze any leftovers in an airtight container for up to 3 months. Reheat until piping hot.*

- *To get ahead, you can marinate the chicken overnight or the morning before cooking.*

KIDS'
FAVE

Barbecued Steak Fajitas

Here's a quick summer meal that you can cook up on the barbie.
I like to marinate the steak and cut up the veggies earlier in
the day so it comes together quickly at dinnertime.

Chipotle Mayo

¼ cup mayonnaise
1 Tbsp chipotle sauce
a squeeze of lime juice

500 g (1 lb 2 oz) rump or
  sirloin steak
1 Tbsp olive oil
1 tsp ground cumin
1 tsp smoked paprika
½ tsp salt
1 red onion, cut into thin
  wedges
1 red capsicum, finely sliced
1 yellow capsicum, finely
  sliced
8 tortillas

To serve

flesh of 2 avocados, sliced
fresh coriander
chilli flakes
lime wedges

1. To make the Chipotle Mayo, combine the ingredients in a small bowl and chill until needed.

2. Place the steak in a bowl. Add the oil, cumin, smoked paprika and salt and turn the steak to coat.

3. Grill the steak on a hot barbecue for a few minutes on each side, until cooked to your liking. Allow to rest for a few minutes, then carve into thin slices.

4. Barbecue the onion and capsicums on the flat griddle for about 10 minutes, until cooked through.

5. Just before serving, toast the tortillas on the barbecue for about 1 minute on each side.

6. Serve warm, topped with the grilled steak, onion, capsicums and avocado slices. Drizzle with Chipotle Mayo and garnish with coriander and chilli flakes. Serve lime wedges alongside.

Tips and tricks

- *The steak could be swapped out for chicken if you prefer. Just make sure it is cooked through before serving.*

Quick Smoked Salmon Pasta with Capers

This tasty, zesty pasta comes together fast, so it's a good idea to prep the ingredients first. Then all you have to do is combine them in the frying pan and serve.

400 g (14 oz) dried
  fettuccine
2 Tbsp butter
1 Tbsp olive oil
3 Tbsp capers
4 cloves garlic, finely sliced
¼ tsp chilli flakes (optional)
1 cup cream
finely grated zest of 1 lemon
3 Tbsp lemon juice
200 g (7 oz) hot-smoked
  salmon, flaked
salt and cracked black
  pepper, to taste
2 Tbsp finely chopped fresh
  parsley, to serve
lemon wedges, to serve

1. Cook the pasta according to the packet instructions until al dente. Drain, reserving 1 cup of pasta cooking water.

2. While the pasta is cooking, melt the butter with the oil in a large frying pan over a low heat. Once it starts to sizzle, add the capers, garlic and chilli (if using). Cook, stirring, for 3 minutes, until the garlic starts to brown.

3. Stir in the cream, lemon zest, lemon juice and ½ cup of the reserved pasta water, and simmer gently until the sauce starts to thicken up.

4. Stir in three-quarters of the smoked salmon.

5. Stir in the drained pasta, adding a little extra pasta water if necessary to loosen the sauce. Season to taste with salt and pepper.

6. Serve garnished with the parsley and the remaining smoked salmon, accompanied by lemon wedges.

Meatball Subs

The beauty of these subs is that you can either make them from scratch with the meatball recipe below, or if you're short on time you can use pre-made meatballs from the supermarket.

500 g (1 lb 2 oz) lean beef mince
¼ cup breadcrumbs
1 small onion, grated
1 egg
2 Tbsp barbecue sauce
1 Tbsp Worcestershire sauce
1 tsp dried mixed herbs
1 tsp garlic powder
½ tsp salt
1 tsp oil, for frying
325 g (11½ oz) tomato pasta sauce

To serve
4 long rolls
1 cup grated cheese
fresh Italian parsley, chopped

1. Preheat the oven to 200°C (400°F) fan grill. Line a baking tray with baking paper.

2. To make the meatballs, place the mince in a large bowl with the breadcrumbs, onion, egg, barbecue sauce, Worcestershire sauce, herbs, garlic powder and salt. Mix together with your hands or a wooden spoon. Shape into 12 large meatballs or 16 smaller meatballs.

3. Heat the oil in a large frying pan and fry the meatballs until nicely browned and cooked through.

4. Add the pasta sauce and cook, stirring, for a few minutes, until heated through.

5. Cut the rolls in half and place them on the prepared tray. Divide the meatballs and sauce between the rolls.

6. Scatter with the cheese, then place under the grill for 10 minutes until the cheese is golden and bubbling.

7. Scatter with parsley and serve immediately.

Tips and tricks
- *Any type of meatballs would work in this recipe.*
- *You can eat these as they are or add your favourite toppings, such as sour cream, mayonnaise, barbecue sauce or fresh salad ingredients.*
- *I like to use the fresh tomato pasta sauces you can find in the chiller at the supermarket.*

KIDS' FAVE

Sweet and Sour Pork

This is my home-made take on the Chinese takeaway favourite.
I shallow-fry the pork but if you want it crispier you can use extra oil
and deep-fry it. I like to serve it on top of steamed rice or noodles.

500 g (1 lb 2 oz) diced pork

½ cup cornflour

1 egg, whisked

120 g (4¼ oz) green beans, trimmed and chopped

400 g (14 oz) can pineapple pieces

3 Tbsp vegetable oil

1 red capsicum, chopped

1 spring onion, finely sliced

1 tsp sesame seeds

Sweet and Sour Sauce

¼ cup apple cider vinegar

3 Tbsp low-salt soy sauce

2 Tbsp tomato sauce

2 Tbsp brown sugar

2 Tbsp crushed garlic

2 Tbsp crushed ginger

1. Coat the pork well in cornflour then add the whisked egg and mix together. Set aside.

2. Place the beans in a small bowl and cover with boiling water. Drain the pineapple, reserving the juice.

3. To make the Sweet and Sour Sauce, measure ¼ cup of the pineapple juice into a bowl or jug. Add the sauce ingredients and whisk to combine.

4. To cook the pork, heat the oil in a large frying pan. Working in batches, add the pork pieces and fry until crispy. Remove from the pan and set aside.

5. Wipe any excess oil out of the frying pan. Drain the beans and add to the pan with the capsicum and 1 cup of the pineapple pieces. Stir-fry for a few minutes until the pineapple starts to brown.

6. Add the Sweet and Sour Sauce and simmer with the vegetables, stirring, for a few minutes. Once it starts to thicken, add the pork and quickly coat it in the sauce.

7. Serve immediately, sprinkled with spring onion and sesame seeds.

Tips and tricks

- *The boiling water starts to cook the green beans so you don't have to stir-fry them for long.*

- *I like to give the leftover pineapple pieces to my kids as a snack or save them to use on a pizza.*

KIDS' FAVE

Southern-style Fried Chicken

I think fried chicken would have to be my favourite food! I make it with this coating all the time and serve it either in burgers or with sides of coleslaw and dinner rolls. My followers love it so much they have nicknamed it Vanya's Fried Chicken or VFC.

1 cup milk
1 Tbsp white vinegar
1 tsp salt
½ tsp ground white pepper
1 kg (2 lb 4 oz) boneless, skinless chicken thighs
1 litre (35 fl oz) oil, for deep-frying

Crispy Coating

1½ cups plain flour
¼ cup cornflour
1 Tbsp paprika
2 tsp garlic powder
1 tsp dried mixed herbs
1 tsp salt
1 tsp ground white pepper

1. Mix the milk, vinegar, salt and pepper in a shallow dish or container. Using tongs, add the chicken and turn to coat. Chill for at least 30 minutes.

2. To make the Crispy Coating, mix the ingredients together in a large bowl.

3. Using clean tongs, pick up a piece of chicken and allow the excess marinade to drip back into the marinade container. Place the chicken in the Crispy Coating and turn to coat completely. Repeat with remaining chicken pieces.

4. Heat the oil in a large cast-iron pot over a high heat. Once hot, carefully lower 2–3 pieces of coated chicken into the oil, allowing room for each piece to cook properly.

5. Fry for 8–10 minutes until golden and cooked through. Transfer to a wire rack to drain. Repeat until all the chicken has been cooked.

Tips and tricks

- *Make sure you use oil with a high smoke point, such as rice bran or canola oil, for deep-frying. Keep an eye on it so it doesn't get too hot, and turn it down between batches if necessary.*

KIDS' FAVE

Vegetarian Lasagne

This recipe makes a huge batch, so you can either make one large lasagne or split it into two medium dishes and pop one in the freezer for later. Serve with a salad for the perfect family meal.

2 purple kūmara, cut into
   1 cm (½ in) slices
½ pumpkin, peeled and cut
   into 1 cm (½ in) slices
5 Tbsp olive oil
2 capsicums, chopped
2 onions, finely diced
2 carrots, finely diced
200 g (7 oz) mushrooms,
   sliced
3 Tbsp tomato paste
1 Tbsp dried Italian herbs
2 x 400g (14 oz) cans
   chopped tomatoes
salt and cracked black
   pepper, to taste
400 g (14 oz) fresh lasagne
   sheets
1 cup grated cheese, for
   topping

White Sauce

50 g (1¾ oz) butter
⅓ cup plain flour
2 cups milk
1 cup grated cheese
1 tsp wholegrain mustard
salt and cracked black
   pepper, to taste

1. Preheat the oven to 200°C (400°F) fan bake. Line 3 baking trays with baking paper.

2. Arrange the kūmara in a single layer on one prepared tray and the pumpkin on another. Drizzle each tray with 1 tablespoon of the oil and season well with salt and pepper. Roast for 40–45 minutes until soft and cooked through.

3. While the kūmara and pumpkin are roasting, arrange the capsicum on the third tray. Drizzle with 1 tablespoon of the oil then roast for 20 minutes until soft.

4. Heat the remaining 2 tablespoons of oil in a large frying pan over a medium heat. Add the onions and carrots and sauté for 10 minutes until soft.

5. Add the mushrooms and fry until soft.

6. Add the tomato paste and Italian herbs and fry off for a few minutes. Stir in the canned tomatoes and simmer for 10 minutes until the liquid has reduced a little. Season to taste with salt and pepper.

7. To make the White Sauce, place a large pot over a low heat and add the butter. Stir until melted, then stir in the flour. Keep stirring for a minute to fry the mixture. Add the milk slowly, stirring between each addition, then simmer gently until thick.

8. Remove from the heat and stir in the cheese and mustard. Season well with salt and pepper.

Continued overleaf...

9. To assemble the lasagne, lightly grease the base of a large oven dish and line it with lasagne sheets. Top with half the tomato sauce, then the kumara and roasted capsicum, then half the white sauce. Add another layer of lasagne sheets, the remaining tomato sauce and the pumpkin, then top with a final layer of lasagne sheets and the remaining white sauce.

10. Top with the extra cheese and bake for 50 minutes, until golden and bubbling. Allow to rest for 10 minutes before serving up.

Tips and tricks
- *Don't reduce the tomato sauce too much. You need a little liquid to soak into the pasta and vegetables.*

Korean Beef on Rice

I'm always on the lookout for new ideas for cooking mince, and
this recipe hits the spot because it's so easy and family-friendly.
I love a quick dinner and this is made in no time at all.

1 Tbsp sesame oil
1 onion, finely diced
1 carrot, finely diced
500 g (1 lb 2 oz) lean
  beef mince
1 Tbsp crushed ginger
2 tsp crushed garlic
¼ cup low-salt soy sauce
2 Tbsp brown sugar
2 tsp apple cider vinegar
1 tsp cornflour
1 beef stock cube
½ cup boiling water
salt and cracked black
  pepper, to taste

To serve

2 cups cooked rice
1 spring onion, sliced
sriracha (optional)

1. Heat the oil in a large frying pan. Add the onion and carrot and cook, stirring, for 5 minutes.

2. Add the mince and cook, breaking up with a wooden spoon, for 5–10 minutes until nicely browned. Add the ginger and garlic, and stir through the mince until fragrant.

3. Mix the soy sauce, sugar, vinegar and cornflour in a small jug. Add to the mince and stir to combine.

4. Dissolve the stock cube in the boiling water. Add to the mince and allow to simmer for a few minutes until the sauce thickens up. Season to taste with salt and pepper.

5. Serve on rice with a garnish of spring onion and a swirl of sriracha on top (if using).

Tips and tricks

- *The stock cube and boiling water can be swapped for ½ cup liquid beef stock.*

- *Beef mince can be swapped for pork or chicken mince.*

KIDS' FAVE

Chicken Parmigiana Tray Bake

There are two ways you can serve this tasty chicken parmigiana: either pub-style with fries and a side salad or Italian-style on top of cooked pasta. Either way will be delicious.

500 g (1 lb 2 oz) chicken breasts
½ cup breadcrumbs
¼ cup finely grated parmesan
1 tsp garlic powder
½ tsp salt
¼ tsp cracked black pepper
¼ cup plain flour
1 egg, whisked
2 Tbsp olive oil
325 g (11½ oz) tomato pasta sauce
200 g (7 oz) mozzarella, sliced
fresh basil or parsley, to serve

1. Preheat the oven to 180°C (350°F) fan grill.

2. Cut the chicken breasts in half horizontally. Place each piece under a sheet of baking paper and flatten with a mallet or rolling pin to an even thickness of about 1.5 cm (⅝ in).

3. Mix the breadcrumbs, parmesan, garlic powder, salt and pepper in a shallow bowl. Place the flour and egg in separate bowls.

4. Coat each piece of chicken in flour, then egg, and finally the breadcrumb mixture.

5. Heat the oil in a frying pan over a medium heat and fry the chicken for 4 minutes on each side, until golden.

6. Pour half the pasta sauce into the base of an oven dish, arrange the chicken on top then spoon the remaining pasta sauce over the chicken. Divide the mozzarella between the chicken pieces.

7. Place under the grill for 10–15 minutes until the mozzarella has melted and the chicken has cooked through.

8. Sprinkle with herbs and serve immediately.

Tips and tricks
- *I like to use the fresh tomato pasta sauces you can find in the chiller at the supermarket.*

Pork Lettuce Cups

If you're looking for a fresh, light dinner you must try these lettuce cups. The kids will love piling the lettuce leaves with fillings and eating them with their hands.

1 tsp vegetable oil
500 g (1 lb 2 oz) pork mince
1 carrot, finely diced or grated
1 tsp crushed garlic
1 tsp crushed ginger
¼ cup hoisin sauce
2 Tbsp low-salt soy sauce
1 Tbsp fish sauce
1 tsp sesame oil

To serve
8 leaves iceberg or cos lettuce
50 g (1¾ oz) bean sprouts
1 spring onion, finely sliced
¼ cup roasted peanuts or cashews
fresh coriander (optional)
Japanese mayonnaise (optional)
sriracha (optional)

1. Heat the vegetable oil in a large frying pan. Add the mince and cook, breaking up with a wooden spoon, for 5 minutes.

2. Stir in the carrot, garlic and ginger, then stir-fry for 3 minutes.

3. Add the hoisin sauce, soy sauce, fish sauce and sesame oil and stir for a few minutes, until everything is cooked through.

4. To serve, fill the lettuce leaves with the mince mixture, then top with bean sprouts, spring onion and nuts. Add extra toppings of your choice, such as coriander, mayonnaise and sriracha, and serve immediately.

Tips and tricks

- *If you want to add some carbs, you can also serve the pork mince mixture on a bowl of rice topped with avocado, lettuce and bean sprouts. Finish with mayo, spring onion and peanuts.*

- *This recipe would work well with beef or chicken mince too.*

Pumpkin, Haloumi and Cauliflower Curry

This vegetarian curry has the perfect balance of flavours, combining salty haloumi and sweet pumpkin. I like to finish it off with a good dollop of thick yoghurt.

400 g (14 oz) can chopped tomatoes
400 ml (14 fl oz) can coconut milk
¼ cup Greek yoghurt
1 tsp honey
2 Tbsp butter
200 g (7 oz) haloumi, diced
1 onion, finely diced
2 cloves garlic, crushed
2 tsp curry powder
2 tsp garam masala
2 tsp mild yellow curry paste
½ head cauliflower, cut into small florets
400 g (14 oz) peeled and chopped pumpkin
1 Tbsp lemon juice
salt and cracked black pepper, to taste

To serve
3 cups cooked rice
⅓ cup Greek yoghurt
fresh coriander or parsley

1. Blitz the canned tomatoes, coconut milk, yoghurt and honey in a blender until smooth. Set aside.

2. Melt 1 tablespoon of the butter in a non-stick frying pan. Add the haloumi and cook until nicely browned. Remove from the pan and set aside.

3. Add the second tablespoon of butter to the pan, then add the onion and garlic. Cook over a gentle heat for 5 minutes, until soft.

4. Add the curry powder, garam masala and yellow curry paste to the pan. Cook for 1 minute, then pour in the tomato mixture and bring to a simmer.

5. Add the haloumi, cauliflower and pumpkin to the pan. Simmer for 30 minutes until the cauliflower has softened and the pumpkin has cooked though. Stir in the lemon juice and season to taste with salt and pepper.

6. Serve the curry on rice topped with yoghurt and coriander or parsley.

Tips and tricks
- *Cauliflower could be swapped for broccoli or green beans.*

Beef and Noodle Stir-fry

This recipe uses my go-to stir-fry sauce, which is so versatile and can be used with any type of meat or even tofu. Beef strips cook fast, so this meal is ready in minutes.

400 g (14 oz) thin egg noodles

1 Tbsp vegetable oil

400 g (14 oz) beef stir-fry strips

½ head broccoli, cut into florets

150 g (5½ oz) green beans, trimmed and chopped

1 red capsicum, sliced

a splash of water

1 tsp sesame seeds, to serve

Stir-fry Sauce

¼ cup low-salt soy sauce

3 Tbsp sweet chilli sauce

1 Tbsp brown sugar

1 Tbsp sesame oil

1 Tbsp cornflour

1 tsp crushed garlic

1 tsp crushed ginger

1. Cook the noodles according to the packet instructions. Drain and set aside.

2. To make the Stir-fry Sauce, whisk the ingredients together in a small jug. Set aside.

3. Heat the oil in a large non-stick frying pan. Add the beef strips and fry for a couple of minutes on each side. Remove from the pan and set aside while you cook the vegetables.

4. Add the broccoli, beans, capsicum and water to the pan and stir-fry for 3 minutes.

5. Return the cooked beef to the pan. Add the noodles and Stir-fry Sauce and stir for 2 minutes until hot and cooked through.

6. Scatter with sesame seeds and serve immediately.

Tips and tricks

- *Substitute or add your favourite seasonal vegetables, such as carrot, bok choy, bean sprouts or cauliflower.*

KIDS' FAVE

Moroccan Lamb Pies

Lamb mince is enhanced by fragrant cinnamon and cumin and pops of sweet sultana in these moreish Moroccan parcels. Serve with tomato relish and a side salad.

1 Tbsp olive oil
1 onion, finely diced
500 g (1 lb 2 oz) lamb mince
1 tsp crushed garlic
1 tsp ground cumin
½ tsp cinnamon
½ tsp salt
½ cup sultanas, chopped
¼ cup tomato relish
1 cup water
3 sheets puff pastry
1 egg, whisked
1 tsp sesame seeds

1. Heat the oil in a large frying pan and sauté the onion for a few minutes, until soft.

2. Add the lamb mince and cook, breaking up with a wooden spoon, until nicely browned. Drain off any excess fat.

3. Stir in the garlic, cumin, cinnamon and salt, then the sultanas and tomato relish.

4. Add the water and simmer for 5–10 minutes, until the liquid has reduced and the mince is cooked through.

5. Allow to cool slightly, or chill overnight, before making the pies.

6. Preheat the oven to 200°C (400°F) fan bake.

7. Cut each pastry sheet into 4 squares. Divide the filling between the 12 squares, then pull up the corners of each square and pinch the seams together on top.

8. Brush the egg over the pies. Sprinkle with sesame seeds and bake for 25 minutes until golden and crispy.

Tips and tricks

- *This recipe can also be made as one large pie, 6 medium pies or even mini pies for a party.*

- *If you don't allow the mince mixture to cool first, it can make the pastry soggy.*

KIDS' FAVE

One-pot Chicken and Lemon Orzo

One-pot chicken is one of my signature dishes — baking chicken thighs gives them so much flavour. I also love how the orzo cooks in the sauce, soaking up the beautiful garlic and lemon flavours. Too easy!

500 g (1 lb 2 oz) boneless
  chicken thighs
2 Tbsp olive oil
1 tsp ground cumin
1 tsp mixed herbs
salt and cracked black
  pepper, to season
1 lemon, sliced
2 Tbsp butter
3 cloves garlic, finely sliced
1 cup dried orzo pasta
2 chicken stock cubes
2 cups boiling water
1 capsicum, finely sliced
70 g (2½ oz) baby spinach
  leaves
½ cup cream
fresh basil, to serve

1. Preheat the oven to 180°C (350°F) fan bake.

2. Cut each chicken thigh into thirds. Mix 1 tablespoon of the oil with the cumin, mixed herbs and the salt and pepper in a large bowl. Add the chicken and turn to coat.

3. Heat the remaining 1 tablespoon of oil in a large casserole dish or ovenproof frying pan over a medium heat. Add the chicken and brown for a few minutes on each side. Remove from the pan and set aside.

4. Add the lemon slices to the pan and fry for 1 minute on each side to brown. Remove from the pan and set aside with the chicken.

5. Reduce the heat to low and add the butter. Once the butter is melted and bubbling, add the garlic and cook, stirring, for 2 minutes, until it just starts to brown. Add the orzo and cook for about 2 minutes, until it starts to brown and is coated in the butter.

6. Dissolve the stock cubes in the boiling water. Add to the pan and stir with a wooden spoon to deglaze (release any caramelised bits stuck to the bottom of the pan).

7. Add the capsicum and spinach and stir until the spinach wilts.

8. Add the chicken and any resting juices back into the dish. Arrange the browned lemon slices on top.

Continued overleaf . . .

9. Bake uncovered for 15 minutes.

10. Remove from the oven and gently stir in the cream. Season to taste with salt and pepper.

11. Return to the oven for a further 5 minutes, until the top is golden and the chicken is cooked through.

12. Top with basil and serve immediately.

Tips and tricks

- *In a recipe like this, chicken thighs work better than chicken breasts, which could dry out.*

- *Orzo is sometimes called risoni in supermarkets.*

- *The stock cubes and boiling water can be swapped for 2 cups liquid chicken stock.*

Salads to Impress

What's in this Chapter

**Thai Beef
Salad** p96

**Mexican Chicken
Salad** p98

**Roasted Vegetable
Couscous Salad** p100

**Chicken Caesar
Salad** p102

**Raw Broccoli
Salad** p106

**Barbecued Zucchini Salad
with Feta Whip** p108

**Prawn Cocktail
Salad** p110

**Asian Slaw with
Crispy Noodles** p112

**Avocado, Corn, Tomato
and Black Bean Salad** p114

**Salmon and Warm
Potato Salad** p116

Thai Beef Salad

I made a double recipe of this salad when we went to a beach house for my friend's hen party. I made the dressing at home and took it along in a jar. The rest of it was so simple to make and everyone was so impressed.

Thai Dressing
¼ cup low-salt soy sauce
2 Tbsp fish sauce
2 Tbsp lime juice
2 Tbsp brown sugar
2 tsp sesame oil
2 cloves garlic, crushed
1 tsp crushed ginger

600 g (1 lb 5 oz) rump steak
1 Tbsp olive oil
salt and cracked black
  pepper, to season
100 g (3½ oz) vermicelli
  noodles
130 g (4½ oz) mesclun
100 g (3½ oz) sugar snap
  peas, finely sliced
100 g (3½ oz) bean sprouts
½ cucumber, finely sliced
½ red capsicum, finely sliced
½ red onion, finely sliced
½ cup chopped fresh mint
¼ cup crushed roasted
  peanuts

1. To make the Thai Dressing, whisk the ingredients in a small jug. Chill until needed.

2. Coat the steak in the oil then season with salt and pepper.

3. Heat a frying pan or barbecue to a high heat and cook the steak for 2–4 minutes on each side until done to your liking. Allow to rest while you prepare the salad, then carve into thin strips.

4. Cook the noodles according to the packet instructions. Drain well.

5. To assemble the salad, arrange the noodles and mesclun on a large serving platter. Scatter with the sugar snaps, bean sprouts, cucumber, capsicum and onion.

6. Top with the steak strips, mint and peanuts.

7. Drizzle with some of the dressing just before serving. Leave the rest in a jug on the side so each person can add extra.

Tips and tricks
- *Cook the steak to your preference and that of your guests. Medium rare is nice and tender.*

Mexican Chicken Salad

The way you present a meal can transform a simple recipe into something spectacular. Here, it's all about the way you layer up the ingredients. I have a few different large platters that are perfect for serving salads like this.

Chipotle Dressing
½ cup thick mayo
1½ Tbsp chipotle sauce
1 Tbsp lemon or lime juice
¼ tsp paprika
¼ tsp salt

1 cup brown rice
800 g (1 lb 12 oz) chicken breasts
2 Tbsp olive oil
1 Tbsp ground cumin
1 Tbsp paprika
1 tsp salt
2 corn cobs
1 iceberg lettuce, chopped
200 g (7 oz) cherry tomatoes, halved
100 g (3½ oz) plain corn chips
flesh of 3 avocados, sliced
1 spring onion, finely sliced
2 Tbsp chopped fresh coriander (optional)

1. To make the Chipotle Dressing, whisk the ingredients in a small bowl. Chill until needed.

2. Cook the rice according to the packet instructions. Allow to cool.

3. Cut the chicken breasts in half horizontally. Whisk the oil, cumin, paprika and salt in a large dish, add the chicken and turn to coat. Chill until needed.

4. Heat a barbecue grill or large frying pan to a high heat, add the chicken and cook for about 4 minutes on each side, until cooked through. Grill the corn cobs at the same time.

5. Allow the chicken to rest while you slice the corn kernels off the cobs and assemble the salad.

6. Arrange the lettuce on a large serving platter, then scatter with the rice, corn kernels, tomatoes and corn chips.

7. Slice the chicken and arrange on top of the salad, along with the avocado slices. Scatter with the spring onion and coriander (if using).

8. Drizzle some Chipotle Dressing over the salad and serve the rest in a jug on the side.

Tips and tricks
- *To get ahead, the chicken can be marinated the day before.*
- *I like to microwave corn cobs with the husks on for 3 minutes before grilling them on the barbecue.*

KIDS' FAVE

Roasted Vegetable Couscous Salad

It seems like I'm always making different variations on this salad. I love the combo of salty feta with sweet roasted vegetables and earthy couscous. It's ideal to take to a barbecue because it transports well and feeds a crowd.

½ head cauliflower, cut into small florets
2 carrots, peeled and chopped
1 kūmara, chopped
1 red capsicum, chopped
1 red onion, chopped
1 Tbsp olive oil
salt and cracked black pepper, to season
1 vegetable stock cube
1½ cups boiling water
1 cup couscous
1 cup baby spinach leaves
100 g (3½ oz) feta

Creamy Pesto Dressing
3 Tbsp pesto
1 Tbsp mayonnaise
1 Tbsp olive oil
1 Tbsp lime juice
salt and cracked black pepper, to taste

1. Preheat the oven to 200°C (400°F) fan bake. Line 2 baking trays with baking paper.

2. Arrange the cauliflower, carrots, kūmara, capsicum and onion in a single layer on the prepared trays. Drizzle with oil then season well with salt and pepper.

3. Roast for 30 minutes, until golden brown and cooked through.

4. While the vegetables are roasting, prepare the couscous. Dissolve the stock cube in the boiling water in a large bowl, stir in the couscous then cover and allow to sit for 10 minutes before fluffing with a fork.

5. Make the Creamy Pesto Dressing by mixing the ingredients in a small bowl or jug.

6. To assemble the salad, transfer the warm couscous to a large serving platter, then stir in the spinach. Scatter with the roasted vegetables and crumble over the feta, then drizzle with Creamy Pesto Dressing.

Tips and tricks
- *The stock cube and boiling water can be swapped for 1½ cups liquid vegetable stock.*

Chicken Caesar Salad

Serve this salad as a side or divide it between four bowls for lunch or a light dinner. The home-made Caesar dressing nails the flavour — you'll love it!

Caesar Dressing

½ cup cream
¼ cup mayonnaise
¼ cup finely grated parmesan
1 clove garlic, crushed
2 Tbsp olive oil
1 Tbsp lemon juice
1 tsp Worcestershire sauce
½ tsp mustard

2 bread rolls
2 Tbsp olive oil
500 g (1 lb 2 oz) chicken
  breasts
salt and cracked black
  pepper, to season
250 g (9 oz) bacon, chopped
2 heads cos lettuce, chopped
2 Tbsp shaved parmesan

1. Preheat the oven to 200°C (400°F) fan bake.

2. To make the Caesar Dressing, whisk the ingredients in a small jug. Chill until needed.

3. Cut the bread rolls into small pieces and toss on a lined baking tray with 1 tablespoon of the oil. Bake for 12 minutes until golden and crunchy.

4. Cut the chicken breasts in half horizontally. Drizzle with the remaining 1 tablespoon of oil and season well with salt and pepper.

5. Heat a frying pan over a high heat and cook the chicken for 5 minutes on each side, until cooked through. Transfer to a plate and allow to rest for a few minutes, then cut into bite-size pieces.

6. Add the bacon to the same pan and fry until crispy.

7. Place the lettuce, chicken and croutons in a large bowl. Add the Caesar Dressing and toss to coat.

8. Transfer to a large serving platter and scatter with bacon and parmesan to serve.

Tips and tricks

- *Poached eggs would make a lovely addition to this salad.*

- *If you are taking this to a barbecue, put the dressing in a separate container and coat the salad just before serving.*

Raw Broccoli Salad

I guarantee everyone who tries this salad will ask you for the recipe.
The crispy bacon is optional if you prefer a vegetarian version.

2 heads broccoli, finely
   chopped
1 spring onion, finely sliced
½ cup dried cranberries
½ cup pine nuts, toasted
½ cup Greek yoghurt
½ cup thick mayonnaise
1 Tbsp lemon juice
salt and cracked black
   pepper, to taste
crispy bacon, to serve
   (optional)

1. Combine the broccoli, spring onion, cranberries and pine nuts in a salad bowl, reserving a teaspoon each of the cranberries and pine nuts for the garnish.

2. To make the dressing, mix the yoghurt, mayonnaise, lemon juice and the salt and pepper in a small bowl or jug.

3. Add the dressing to the salad and toss to combine. Chill until needed.

4. Serve sprinkled with the reserved cranberries and pine nuts and the crispy bacon (if using).

Tips and tricks
- *This salad can be made a day ahead of time and chilled until needed.*

Barbecued Zucchini Salad with Feta Whip

Salty, creamy whipped feta is the perfect base for the sweet
smokiness of barbecued vegetables and a tangy balsamic glaze.
You won't believe how easy it is to whip up (haha).

2 zucchini, cut into strips
1 capsicum, finely sliced
1 red onion, cut into wedges
1 Tbsp olive oil
salt and cracked black
  pepper, to season
30 g (1 oz) rocket or baby
  spinach leaves
¼ cup pine nuts, toasted
1 Tbsp balsamic glaze

Feta Whip
100 g (3½ oz) Greek yoghurt
50 g (1¾ oz) feta
1 Tbsp lemon juice
salt and cracked black
  pepper, to taste

1. Place the zucchini, capsicum and onion in a bowl with the oil and the salt and pepper. Toss to coat.

2. Grill the vegetables on a hot barbecue until slightly charred and cooked through.

3. To make the Feta Whip, mix the ingredients until smooth.

4. To serve, spread the Feta Whip on the base of a platter. Top with the rocket or spinach and the grilled vegetables. Scatter with the pine nuts and drizzle with the balsamic glaze.

Tips and tricks
- *The pine nuts could be swapped for toasted almonds or sunflower seeds.*

Prawn Cocktail Salad

This salad is my modern interpretation of a 1980s prawn cocktail.
I make it as a special treat during the festive season.

Marie Rose Dressing
½ cup mayonnaise
3 Tbsp tomato sauce
1 Tbsp lime juice
2 tsp Worcestershire sauce
½ tsp paprika

1 head cos lettuce, leaves
  separated and torn if large
flesh of 3 avocados, sliced
2 Tbsp garlic butter
500 g (1 lb 2 oz) cooked
  and peeled jumbo prawns,
  thawed if frozen
lime wedges, to serve
chilli flakes, to serve
  (optional)

1. To make the Marie Rose Dressing, mix together the ingredients in a small bowl or jug. Chill until needed.

2. To assemble the salad, arrange the lettuce on a large serving platter, then arrange the avocado slices on top.

3. Melt the garlic butter in a large frying pan, until sizzling. Add the prawns and fry for 1 minute on each side. Arrange on top of the lettuce and avocado.

4. Serve drizzled with Marie Rose Dressing and accompanied by lime wedges. Sprinkle with chilli flakes (if using).

Tips and tricks
- *This recipe can easily be halved to serve as a special dinner for two.*
- *You can find big bags of frozen jumbo prawns at the supermarket.*

Asian Slaw with Crispy Noodles

I found this recipe in one of my old recipe notebooks, circled in pen with a big note saying 'Delicious!' Here I've made it with a mixture of red and green cabbage, but you can use whatever you have on hand. My favourite noodles are the crispy ones from the Asian specialty stores.

Miso Dressing

3 Tbsp Japanese mayonnaise
2 Tbsp olive oil
1 Tbsp miso paste
1 Tbsp low-salt soy sauce
1 Tbsp runny honey
1 Tbsp rice wine vinegar
1 tsp sesame oil

¼ cup pumpkin seeds
1 tsp low-salt soy sauce
¼ green cabbage
¼ red cabbage
3 carrots, peeled
3 spring onions
1 handful crispy noodles

1. To make the Miso Dressing, whisk together the ingredients in a small bowl or jug. Chill while you prepare the salad.

2. Gently heat the pumpkin seeds in a small non-stick frying pan until they start to brown. Add the soy sauce and remove from the heat, gently stirring the soy sauce through the seeds as it dries in the pan. Transfer to a plate to cool.

3. To make the slaw, use a mandoline or a food processor to finely shred the cabbage, carrots and spring onions. Place in a large serving bowl with the crispy noodles.

4. Add the Miso Dressing and toss to combine.

5. Sprinkle with the pumpkin seeds to serve.

Tips and tricks
- *To prep this slaw ahead of time, prepare the vegetables then add the crispy noodles, dressing and pumpkin seeds just before serving.*

Avocado, Corn, Tomato and Black Bean Salad

This quick and colourful salad is a handy way to make something zesty and fresh with canned corn and beans. The lime dressing and jalapeños take it to the next level.

Lime Dressing

¼ cup olive oil

2 tsp runny honey

finely grated zest of 1 lime

2 Tbsp lime juice

salt and cracked black
  pepper, to taste

400 g (14 oz) can black
  beans, rinsed and drained

400 g (14 oz) can whole corn
  kernels, drained

200 g (7 oz) cherry
  tomatoes, halved

flesh of 1 large avocado,
  diced

2 Tbsp chives, finely chopped

2 Tbsp jalapeños, finely
  chopped (optional)

fresh coriander, to serve

1. To make the Lime Dressing, place the ingredients in a small bowl or jug and whisk until the mixture starts to lighten in colour slightly.

2. To make the salad, combine the beans and corn in a large bowl.

3. Add the tomatoes, avocado, chives and jalapeños (if using) and mix gently to combine.

4. Add the Lime Dressing and mix until coated.

5. Serve sprinkled with coriander.

Tips and tricks

- *If fresh corn is in season I like to use it instead of canned corn. Cook it first, then slice the kernels off the cob.*

Salmon and Warm Potato Salad

I'm a big fan of potato salad, especially this version. It's topped with tasty salmon pieces and loads of green veggies, so you can enjoy it as a main or a side.

400 g (14 oz) salmon fillet
2 Tbsp sweet chilli sauce
500 g (1 lb 2 oz) small new
   potatoes
½ bunch (about 6 stalks)
   asparagus, chopped
½ cup edamame beans
1 head cos lettuce, chopped
1 cucumber, sliced
flesh of 1 avocado, diced
1 spring onion, sliced
fresh basil, to serve

Pesto Dressing
3 Tbsp pesto
3 Tbsp mayonnaise
1 Tbsp olive oil
1 Tbsp lime juice
salt and cracked black
   pepper, to taste

1. Preheat the oven to 180°C (350°F) fan bake. Line a baking tray with baking paper.

2. Slice the salmon into 4 thin strips, place them on the prepared tray and brush with the sweet chilli sauce. Bake for 15 minutes, until just cooked through.

3. Meanwhile, boil the potatoes in a large pot of salted water for about 20 minutes, until just cooked. Steam the asparagus and edamame beans over the boiling pot for 5 minutes, until just cooked. Drain the potatoes.

4. To make the Pesto Dressing, whisk the ingredients in a small bowl or jug. Set aside.

5. To assemble the salad, arrange the lettuce on a large serving platter. Top with the potatoes, asparagus, edamame, cucumber, avocado and spring onion. Drizzle with the Pesto Dressing.

6. Cut the cooked salmon into bite-size pieces, discarding the skin. Arrange it on top of the salad.

7. Garnish with basil and serve while warm.

Tips and tricks
· *If asparagus is not in season, I like to use green beans instead.*

Home
Baking

What's in this Chapter

Crispy Cashew
Caramel Slice p122

Chocolate Banana
Cake p124

Lemon and Blueberry
Loaf p126

Lolly Slice p128

The Easiest
Cheese Scones p130

Marshmallow
Brownie Slice p132

Date Loaf p134

Chocolate Fish
Slice p138

Ginger Crunch
Slice p140

**Upside-down
Plum Cake** p142

**Rocky Road
Four Ways** p144

**Chocolate
Muffins** p146

**Seed and Nut
Bars** p148

**Chocolate Rice
Bubble Slice** p150

**Triple Chocolate
Cookies** p152

**Red Velvet
Brownies** p154

**Bliss Balls
Four Ways** p156

Crispy Cashew Caramel Slice

If you have a sweet tooth or are a big caramel fan, you can double the caramel layer in this recipe. The cashews and rice bubbles make a tasty, crispy base.

200 g (7 oz) butter
½ cup white sugar
2 Tbsp golden syrup
1½ cups self-raising flour
1½ cups rice bubbles
1 cup roasted cashews,
   chopped

Caramel Filling

395 g (14 oz) can sweetened
   condensed milk
2 Tbsp butter
2 Tbsp golden syrup

Chocolate Layer

200 g (7 oz) milk or dark
   chocolate
1 Tbsp vegetable oil

1. Preheat the oven to 170°C (325°F) fan bake. Line a 27 x 17 cm (10¾ x 6½ in) slice tin with baking paper.

2. To make the base, place the butter, sugar and golden syrup in a large microwave-proof bowl and microwave until melted. Stir to combine.

3. Stir in the flour, rice bubbles and cashews.

4. Transfer to the prepared tin and press out to the edges. Bake for 10 minutes.

5. While the base is baking, make the Caramel Filling by combining the ingredients in a pot and stirring over a low heat until smooth.

6. Spread the hot Caramel Filling over the base, then return the slice to the oven and bake for a further 15 minutes. Allow to cool in the tin.

7. To make the Chocolate Layer, place the chocolate in a microwave-proof bowl and microwave in bursts until melted. Add the oil and whisk until smooth. Spread over the cooled slice.

8. Chill until the topping has set, then cut into 20 bars. Store in an airtight container in the fridge.

Chocolate Banana Cake

This is my go-to cake for family birthdays. It's so easy to make and a great way to use up brown bananas. I'll often double the recipe so I can make a batch of muffins at the same time.

100 g (3½ oz) butter, melted
1 cup white sugar
1 egg
1 tsp vanilla essence
1 banana, mashed
½ cup natural yoghurt or
  sour cream
1½ cups plain flour
¼ cup cocoa powder
1 tsp baking powder
a pinch of salt
1 tsp baking soda
½ cup boiling water

Chocolate Icing

1 cup icing sugar
1 Tbsp cocoa powder
50 g (1¾ oz) butter, softened
1½ Tbsp boiling water

1. Preheat the oven to 180°C (350°F) fan bake. Line a 22 cm (8½ in) round cake tin with baking paper.

2. Mix together the butter, sugar, egg and vanilla in a large bowl. Stir in the banana and yoghurt.

3. Sift in the flour, cocoa, baking powder and salt, then stir to combine.

4. Dissolve the baking soda in the boiling water. Fold into the cake batter until just combined.

5. Transfer the batter to the prepared tin. Bake for 30–40 minutes, until a skewer inserted into the centre comes out clean. Allow to cool.

6. To make the Chocolate Icing, sift the icing sugar and cocoa into a bowl. Add the butter and boiling water and whisk, adding more water if required, until smooth. Spread over the cooled cake.

KIDS' FAVE

Lemon and Blueberry Loaf

This is a lovely, light loaf, perfect for morning tea.
The lemon glaze looks so pretty with the blueberries.

150 g (5½ oz) butter, melted
1 cup white sugar
1 Tbsp finely grated lemon
  zest
½ cup lemon juice
2 eggs, whisked
2 cups plain flour
1 tsp baking powder
1 tsp baking soda
¾ cup frozen blueberries,
  thawed

Lemon Glaze
1 cup icing sugar
1 tsp finely grated lemon zest
2 Tbsp lemon juice
1–2 tsp boiling water

1. Preheat the oven to 170°C (325°F) fan bake. Line a 27 x 13 cm (10¾ x 5 in) loaf tin with baking paper.

2. Mix together the butter and sugar in a large bowl. Stir in the lemon zest and juice. Add the eggs and mix again.

3. Sift in the flour, baking powder and soda. Fold together until just combined.

4. Pour a third of the batter into the lined tin. Scatter half of the blueberries on top. Repeat with a third more of the mixture and the remaining blueberries. Finish with the remaining loaf mixture and smooth the top.

5. Bake for 50–60 minutes, until a skewer inserted into the centre comes out clean. Allow to cool.

6. To make the Lemon Glaze, mix the icing sugar, lemon zest and juice. Add the boiling water a little at a time until a drizzling consistency is achieved.

7. Drizzle the Lemon Glaze over the cooled loaf. Allow to set before slicing and serving. Store in an airtight container in the pantry.

Tips and tricks
• *You can use fresh blueberries if they are in season.*

Lolly Slice

Lolly cake brings back so many memories of childhood parties.
Lolly slice is even easier to make, because you just need to press
the mixture into a slice tin and scatter coconut over the top.
Watch this yummy treat get snapped up by kids and adults alike!

120 g (4½ oz) butter, melted
½ cup sweetened condensed
  milk
250 g (9 oz) packet malt
  biscuits, crushed
150 g (5½ oz) fruit puffs or
  Explorers, chopped
¼ cup desiccated coconut

1. Line a 20 cm (8 in) square slice tin with baking paper.

2. Place the butter and condensed milk in a large microwave-proof bowl and microwave until melted.

3. Stir in the crushed biscuits and fruit puffs or Explorers.

4. Transfer to the prepared tin and spread out to the edges, pressing down firmly with the back of a spoon. Sprinkle the coconut over the top.

5. Chill for at least 2 hours or overnight until set. Cut into 24 pieces. Store in an airtight container in the fridge.

Tips and tricks
- *You can speed up the setting process by putting the slice in the freezer for 20 minutes.*

KIDS' FAVE

The Easiest Cheese Scones

Everyone needs a classic cheese scone recipe. I have kept these simple so you can pimp them however you like by adding herbs, ham, salami or sun-dried tomatoes. Serve warm with butter.

3 cups plain flour
1 Tbsp baking powder
1 tsp salt
2 cups grated tasty cheese
1 cup soda water
½ cup milk, plus extra for brushing

1. Preheat the oven 200°C (400°F) fan bake. Line a baking tray with baking paper.

2. Sift the flour, baking powder and salt into a large bowl. Add 1½ cups of the cheese and mix to combine.

3. Add the soda water and milk and mix to combine, using your hands to bring it together at the end.

4. Turn out onto a floured surface and shape into a rectangle about 3 cm (1¼ in) thick. Cut into 12 even pieces.

5. Transfer each piece to the lined tray, leaving a little room between pieces. Brush with a little extra milk then scatter with the remaining ½ cup of cheese.

6. Bake for 12–15 minutes until golden and cooked through.

Marshmallow Brownie Slice

This slice is based on one I fell in love with in a café and just had to recreate at home. The brownie base is rich and fudgy, offset perfectly by the creamy chocolate topping and fluffy marshmallows. Everyone enjoys this slice!

100 g (3½ oz) butter
1 cup caster sugar
2 eggs
½ tsp vanilla essence
⅓ cup plain flour
½ cup cocoa powder
½ tsp baking powder

Marshmallow Topping
250 g (9 oz) milk chocolate
1 Tbsp coconut oil
200 g (7 oz) marshmallows

1. Preheat the oven to 150°C (300°F) fan bake. Line a 20 cm (8 in) square slice tin with baking paper.

2. To make the base, place the butter in a large microwave-proof bowl and microwave until melted. Add the sugar, eggs and vanilla and whisk until smooth.

3. Sift in the flour, cocoa and baking powder, then gently fold together until combined.

4. Transfer to the prepared tin and bake for 25 minutes. Allow to cool for at least 15 minutes.

5. To make the Marshmallow Topping, break the chocolate into a large microwave-proof bowl, add the coconut oil and microwave for 45 seconds, until melted. Stir to combine. Allow to cool for 5 minutes, then stir in the marshmallows.

6. Pour onto the cooled base and spread out to the edges. Chill for at least 2 hours or overnight until set.

7. Slice into pieces and serve. Store in an airtight container in the pantry.

Tips and tricks

- *I like the flavour of the coconut oil, but if it's not to your liking you can swap it for a mild-flavoured oil.*

- *Gluten-free flour can be used instead of the plain flour.*

Date Loaf

I discovered this easy date loaf recipe when I first moved to Taupō. A kindy mum made it for me on a playdate and I told her I had to have the recipe. It was scribbled on a tiny piece of paper so I had to do a few tests to get the ingredient amounts right, but now it turns out perfectly every time.

4 Weet-Bix, crushed
1 cup pitted dates, chopped
1 cup white sugar
50 g (1¾ oz) butter, melted
1 tsp baking powder
1 tsp baking soda
1 cup boiling water
1 egg, whisked
1 cup plain flour
1 Tbsp brown sugar

1. Preheat the oven to 180°C (350°F) fan bake. Line a 27 x 13 cm (10¾ x 5 in) loaf tin with baking paper.

2. Combine the Weet-Bix, dates, white sugar, butter, baking powder and baking soda in a large bowl. Add the boiling water and allow to sit for 5 minutes.

3. Stir in the egg. Sift in the flour and fold together until just combined.

4. Transfer to the prepared tin and scatter the top with the brown sugar.

5. Bake for 45–55 minutes, until golden and cooked through.

6. Allow to cool in the tin for at least 10 minutes before turning out onto a wire rack.

7. Serve warm with butter. Store in an airtight container in the pantry.

Chocolate Fish Slice

Everyone loves a hedgehog slice, and I knew this one would
be even more of a hit with the cute chocolate fish on top.
I like to cut it so that each piece has its own fish.

250 g (9 oz) butter
1 cup brown sugar
¼ cup cocoa powder
½ cup milk
1 tsp vanilla essence
2 x 250 g (9 oz) packets wine
  biscuits, crushed
16 mini chocolate fish

Chocolate Topping
2 cups icing sugar
2 Tbsp cocoa powder
2 Tbsp butter, melted
1–2 Tbsp boiling water

1. Line a 27 x 17 cm (10¾ x 6½ in) slice tin with baking paper.

2. Mix together the butter, sugar and cocoa in a large pot over
   a medium heat, until the butter has melted and the sugar
   has dissolved.

3. Remove from the heat and stir in the milk and vanilla, then
   the crushed biscuits.

4. Transfer to the prepared tin and press out to the edges (you
   may have to use your hands for this). Smooth the top with
   the back of a spoon. Chill while you make the topping.

5. To make the Chocolate Topping, combine the icing sugar
   and cocoa in a bowl. Stir in the butter, adding boiling water
   as needed to loosen the mixture, and whisk out any lumps.

6. Spread the Chocolate Topping evenly over the biscuit base
   and arrange the chocolate fish on top.

7. Chill for at least 4 hours or overnight before cutting into
   slices. Store in an airtight container in the fridge.

Tips and tricks
- *I've placed the chocolate fish in a grid pattern and cut the slice
  into pieces around them. If you wanted to cut smaller slices,
  you could arrange the chocolate fish randomly over the top
  then cut through them.*

KIDS'
FAVE

Ginger Crunch Slice

My recipe for the Kiwi classic ginger crunch has an oaty base and is topped with a golden syrup and ginger icing. You can add crystallised ginger on top for the ginger lovers.

1 cup self-raising flour
1 Tbsp ground ginger
1 cup rolled oats
1 cup shredded coconut
½ cup brown sugar
160 g (5¾ oz) butter, melted

Ginger Icing
1½ cups icing sugar
125 g (4½ oz) butter, melted
2 Tbsp golden syrup
1 Tbsp ground ginger
½ cup chopped crystallised
ginger (optional)

1. Preheat the oven to 160°C (315°F) fan bake. Line a 27 x 17 cm (10¾ x 6½ in) slice tin with baking paper.

2. Sift the flour and ginger into a large bowl. Add the rolled oats, coconut, brown sugar and butter then mix together.

3. Transfer to the prepared tin and spread out to the edges, pressing down firmly with the back of a spoon.

4. Bake for 15–20 minutes, until light golden.

5. To make the Ginger Icing, whisk together the icing sugar, butter, golden syrup and ground ginger until smooth.

6. Pour onto the warm base and spread out to the edges. Top with crystallised ginger (if using).

7. Allow to cool for about 20 minutes, then chill until set.

8. Once set, cut into 24 pieces. Store in an airtight container in the fridge.

Upside-down Plum Cake

I make two versions of this plum cake, but I think this gluten-free recipe is the best. The ground almonds give it a lovely texture and nutty flavour, which goes so nicely with the tart plums.

Plum Topping

2 Tbsp butter, melted
¼ cup brown sugar
500 g (1 lb 2 oz) plums

1½ cups gluten-free flour
1 cup ground almonds
1 cup white sugar
1 tsp baking powder
1 tsp baking soda
½ tsp cinnamon
¼ tsp ground nutmeg
¼ tsp ground allspice
¼ tsp salt
1 cup milk
100 g (3½ oz) butter, melted
1 egg, whisked

1. Preheat the oven to 170°C (325°F) fan bake. Line a 22 cm (8½ in) round cake tin with baking paper.

2. To make the Plum Topping, pour the butter into the base of the prepared tin then brush it out to cover the base evenly. Sprinkle the brown sugar evenly over the top.

3. Cut the plums into 1 cm (½ in) thick wedges then layer them into the tin until the base is covered.

4. To make the cake, sift the dry ingredients into a large bowl. Make a well in the centre and pour in the milk, butter and egg. Fold together until evenly combined, then gently pour over the plums.

5. Bake for 45 minutes, until the top is golden and a skewer inserted into the centre comes out clean.

6. Allow to cool in the tin for 30 minutes, then invert onto a serving plate and carefully peel off the baking paper.

Tips and tricks

- *You'll need about 8 medium plums, or you could use another type of stone fruit or even canned pear quarters instead.*

- *Serve cold with yoghurt or whipped cream, or warm with ice cream as a dessert.*

Rocky Road Four Ways

This is another fun recipe to get the kids involved in the kitchen. Simply melt the chocolate and add your favourite fillings — you really can't go wrong! Here are a few of my favourite combos that make for great festive gifts. The method for each recipe is the same.

Turkish Delight Rocky Road

200 g (7 oz) milk chocolate, chopped
200 g (7 oz) dark chocolate, chopped
200 g (7 oz) marshmallows, chopped
3 x 55 g (2 oz) Turkish Delight bars, chopped
⅔ cup roasted almonds, chopped

White Chocolate and Cranberry Rocky Road

400 g (14 oz) white chocolate, chopped
100 g (3½ oz) white marshmallows, chopped
1 cup dried cranberries
½ cup shelled pistachios

Caramilk Rocky Road

2 x 180 g (6 oz) bars Caramilk chocolate, chopped
100 g (3½ oz) Maltesers
100 g (3½ oz) white marshmallows, chopped
⅔ cup roasted almonds, chopped

Apricot and Almond Rocky Road

200 g (7 oz) milk chocolate, chopped
100 g (3½ oz) dark chocolate, chopped
200 g (7 oz) marshmallows, chopped
⅔ cup roasted almonds, chopped
⅔ cup dried apricots, chopped

1. Line a 20 cm (8 in) square slice tin with baking paper.

2. Place the chocolate in a large microwave-proof bowl and microwave in 30-second bursts, stirring between bursts, until melted.

3. Add the remaining ingredients and mix to combine.

4. Transfer to the prepared tin, pressing the mix out to the edges.

5. Chill until set then cut into small pieces. Store in an airtight container in the fridge.

KIDS' FAVE

Chocolate Muffins

My kids love chocolate muffins, so I like to make a double batch
and freeze the extras for their lunches. I pop them in the lunchbox
frozen in the morning and they're defrosted by lunchtime.

1 cup white sugar
1 cup milk
½ cup vegetable oil
150 g (5½ oz) butter, melted
2 eggs
1 tsp vanilla essence
2½ cups plain flour
½ cup cocoa powder
1 Tbsp baking powder
1 cup milk chocolate drops

1. Preheat the oven to 190°C (375°F) fan bake. Arrange 12 paper cases in a muffin tin.

2. Whisk together the sugar, milk, oil, butter, eggs and vanilla in a large bowl.

3. Sift in the flour, cocoa and baking powder. Add most of the chocolate drops, reserving a few for the topping. Fold together until just combined.

4. Divide the mixture between the paper cases and top with extra chocolate drops.

5. Bake for 20 minutes, until cooked through.

6. Allow to cool in the tin for a few minutes before transferring to a wire rack to cool completely. Store in an airtight container in the pantry.

Tips and tricks

- *You can swap the milk chocolate drops for white or dark chocolate drops if you like.*

KIDS' FAVE

Seed and Nut Bars

If you've ever eaten a sesame snap, you'll have an idea of how these bars taste. Chewy and crunchy with a subtle honey flavour, they're a great alternative to muesli bars in school lunchboxes.

½ cup sunflower seeds

¼ cup pumpkin seeds

¼ cup sesame seeds

1 cup desiccated coconut

½ cup rice bubbles

½ cup coarsely chopped roasted cashews

½ cup coarsely chopped roasted almonds

100 g (3½ oz) butter

⅔ cup brown sugar

¼ cup honey

1. Line a 27 x 17 cm (10¾ x 6½ in) slice tin with baking paper.

2. Place the sunflower, pumpkin and sesame seeds in a dry frying pan over a gentle heat and toast for 5 minutes, stirring constantly to ensure they don't burn.

3. Transfer to a large mixing bowl and add the coconut, rice bubbles, cashews and almonds. Set aside.

4. Place the butter, sugar and honey in a small pot on a low heat, until melted and bubbling. Continue to bubble for a further 2–3 minutes, stirring constantly.

5. Pour over the dry ingredients and quickly mix to combine.

6. Transfer to the prepared tin and spread out to the edges, pressing down firmly with the back of a spoon.

7. Chill until set then cut into 16 bars. Store in an airtight container in the pantry.

Chocolate Rice Bubble Slice

My twist on the classic rice bubble slice has melted chocolate and dried apricots added. Feel free to swap the apricots for dried cranberries or add your favourite dried fruits, nuts or seeds.

120 g (4¼ oz) butter
½ cup brown sugar
190 g (6¾ oz) milk chocolate
2 Tbsp cocoa powder
3 cups rice bubbles
¼ cup dried apricots, finely chopped
1 tsp sprinkles (optional)

1. Line a 20 cm (8 in) square slice tin with baking paper.

2. Stir the butter and sugar in a large pot over a medium heat until the butter has melted and the sugar has dissolved.

3. Remove from the heat and break in the chocolate. Add the cocoa and stir until the chocolate has melted.

4. Stir in the rice bubbles and apricots.

5. Transfer to the prepared tin and press firmly out to the edges. Smooth the top with the back of a spoon. Scatter with the sprinkles (if using).

6. Chill for at least 2 hours or overnight until set. Cut into 16 squares. Store in an airtight container in the fridge.

KIDS' FAVE

Triple Chocolate Cookies

The recipe for these huge cookies comes from my sister Grace. She is a very talented baker, so I knew we had to have them in this book for everyone to enjoy.

200 g (7 oz) butter
⅔ cup white sugar
⅔ cup brown sugar
1 tsp salt
2 eggs
1 tsp vanilla essence
2 cups plain flour
½ cup cocoa powder
1 tsp baking powder
1 tsp baking soda
½ cup white chocolate
  buttons
½ cup milk chocolate buttons
½ cup dark chocolate buttons
extra chocolate bits
  (optional)

1. Cream the butter, white sugar, brown sugar and salt in a stand mixer until pale and fluffy. Add the eggs, one at a time, beating well after each addition. Beat in the vanilla.

2. Sift the dry ingredients together. Add to the butter mixture and mix to combine.

3. Coarsely chop the chocolate buttons, then stir them into the cookie dough. Chill the dough for 15 minutes.

4. Preheat the oven to 180°C (350°F) fan bake. Line 2 baking trays with baking paper.

5. Scoop or roll the dough into 20 balls and arrange them on the prepared trays, ensuring they are well spaced apart as they will spread out while baking. Press them down slightly, then poke extra chocolate bits (if using) into the dough.

6. Bake for 10–12 minutes (I like to slightly undercook the cookies so that they are quite chewy in the centre). Cool on the tray for a few minutes then transfer to a wire rack to cool completely. Store in an airtight container in the pantry.

Tips and tricks

- *For quick, freshly baked cookies any time, you can freeze the dough balls and store them in a snap-lock bag or airtight container. Just pull them out of the freezer and bake from frozen, adding a few minutes to the baking time to account for the frozen dough.*

- *To make medium cookies, roll the mixture into about 30 balls and bake for 8–10 minutes.*

KIDS' FAVE

READY IN 30 MINUTES × MAKES 16 PIECES

Red Velvet Brownies

These little brownies are super-cute to make for Christmas or Valentine's Day. Oh, who am I kidding? They're irresistible all year round.

150 g (5½ oz) butter, melted
1 cup white sugar
1 egg
2 Tbsp cocoa powder
1 tsp vanilla essence
1–2 tsp red food colouring
1 cup plain flour
½ tsp baking powder
¼ tsp salt
1 tsp white vinegar
100 g (3½ oz) white
  chocolate chips
icing sugar and sprinkles
  (optional), to serve

1. Preheat the oven to 180°C (350°F) fan bake. Line a 20 cm (8 in) square slice tin with baking paper.

2. Whisk the butter and sugar in a large mixing bowl or the bowl of a stand mixer. Add the egg, cocoa, vanilla and food colouring, whisking well after each addition.

3. Add the flour, baking powder and salt, and mix to combine.

4. Mix in the white vinegar. Add the white chocolate chips and mix again.

5. Transfer to the prepared tin and gently smooth out to the edges of the tin.

6. Bake for 25–30 minutes, until crisp on top and just cooked in the centre. Allow to cool in the tin.

7. Cut into 16 pieces or use a cookie cutter to cut into shapes. Dust with icing sugar and sprinkles (if using) to serve. Store in an airtight container in the pantry.

Tips and tricks
- *To make these more festive, use a Christmas tree cookie cutter. They look so cute and make great gifts.*

Bliss Balls Four Ways

Bliss balls are the ultimate home-made treat, sweet enough to satisfy a sugar craving yet full of protein to keep you going. I've suggested four variations here, but feel free to add your favourite nuts, seeds and dried fruit. The method for each recipe is the same.

Cranberry and Almond Bliss Balls

100 g (3½ oz) dark chocolate, chopped
1½ cups dried cranberries
¾ cup desiccated coconut
⅔ cup roasted almonds
¼ cup coconut cream
¼ cup finely chopped roasted almonds, to coat

Weet-Bix and Dark Chocolate Bliss Balls

4 Weet-Bix, crushed
50 g (1¾ oz) dark chocolate, chopped
1½ cups pitted dates
1 cup almonds or cashews
¾ cup desiccated coconut
½ cup coconut cream
¼ cup desiccated coconut, to coat

Peanut Butter and Date Bliss Balls

1 cup pitted dates
1 cup rolled oats
¾ cup sunflower seeds
3 Tbsp peanut butter
3 Tbsp maple syrup
2 Tbsp cocoa powder
¼ cup water
¼ cup finely chopped peanuts, to coat

Apricot and Lemon Bliss Balls

1 cup dried apricots
¾ cup desiccated coconut
⅔ cup roasted cashews
finely grated zest of 1 lemon
1 Tbsp lemon juice
2 tsp honey
¼ cup coconut cream
¼ cup desiccated coconut, to coat

1. Place all the ingredients apart from the coconut cream or water and the coating in a food processor. Blitz until finely ground.

2. Add the coconut cream or water and blitz again until the mixture starts to bind.

3. Roll into 15–20 balls, using about 1 tablespoon of mixture at a time.

4. Place the coating in a small bowl then roll the bliss balls in it to coat well.

5. Store in an airtight container in the fridge.

Desserts

What's in this Chapter

**Passionfruit
Meringue Pie** p162

**Black Forest
Gateau** p164

Peach Galette p168

**Mini Pavlova
Wreath** p170

**Lemon Delicious
Pudding** p174

**Chocolate Whip Cheesecake
Cups with Berries** p176

**Layered White Chocolate
Mud Cake** p178

**Stacked Berry
Pavlova** p182

**Individual Apple
Cobblers** p184

**Brownie
Trifle** p186

**Ginger Kisses
Cheesecake** p190

**Eton Mess
Ambrosia** p192

**Baked Lemon and
Passionfruit Cheesecake**
p194

Passionfruit Meringue Pie

This twist on lemon meringue pie is a great recipe to make when passionfruit are in season. They add a lovely tartness to the creamy filling, which goes so well with the light and crispy meringue topping.

2 sheets sweet short pastry

395 g (14 oz) can sweetened condensed milk

3 egg yolks

1 egg

⅓ cup lemon juice

¼ cup passionfruit pulp

3 egg whites

a pinch of salt

⅔ cup caster sugar

1. Preheat the oven to 200°C (400°F) fan bake. Lightly grease a 22 cm (8½ in) round pie dish.

2. Line the prepared dish with pastry, trimming and discarding any excess. Cover with baking paper, then fill two-thirds with baking beads or dry rice and blind bake for 10 minutes.

3. Remove the baking paper and baking beads or rice. Bake the empty pastry shell for a further 5 minutes then remove from the oven and allow to cool.

4. Reduce the oven temperature to 160°C (315°F).

5. To make the filling, combine the condensed milk, egg yolks, egg, lemon juice and passionfruit pulp in a large bowl. Mix well until smooth and thick, then set aside.

6. To make the meringue, place the egg whites and salt in the bowl of a stand mixer and whisk until soft peaks form. Gradually pour in the sugar, then mix on high speed for 5 minutes, until thick and glossy.

7. Pour the passionfruit mixture into the pastry shell and spread out to the edges. Spoon the meringue evenly over the top and use a fork to create little peaks.

8. Bake for 50 minutes, until the meringue is crispy and golden.

9. Allow to cool for an hour then chill until set. Serve chilled.

Tips and tricks

- *You will need the pulp of about 3 passionfruit to yield ¼ cup. If you can't get fresh passionfruit you can use passionfruit pulp from a can or jar, but it's much sweeter so you may wish to use less pulp and more lemon juice.*

Black Forest Gateau

This is a favourite special-occasion cake in our family, which means I make it several times a year! It looks super-impressive but is actually very easy.

200 ml (7 fl oz) milk
50 g (1¾ oz) butter, diced
½ cup vegetable oil
2 eggs, whisked
2 tsp vanilla essence
2 cups plain flour
¾ cup cocoa powder
2 tsp baking soda
1 tsp baking powder
2 cups white sugar
1 tsp salt
1 tsp instant coffee granules
1 cup boiling water
1¼ cups cream, whipped
30 g (1 oz) dark chocolate,
  grated

Cherry Sauce
2 cups frozen cherries
1 cup frozen mixed berries
¼ cup white sugar
½ cup water

Chocolate Ganache
120 g (4¼ oz) dark chocolate
½ cup cream

1. Preheat the oven to 170°C (325°F) fan bake. Grease two 22 cm (8½ in) round cake tins and line with baking paper.

2. To make the cake batter, place the milk and butter in a large microwave-proof bowl and microwave for 30–40 seconds, until the butter has melted.

3. Stir in the oil, eggs and vanilla. Sift in the flour, cocoa, baking soda and baking powder. Add the sugar and salt and stir to combine.

4. Dissolve the instant coffee in the boiling water. Add to the batter and stir to combine. Whisk out any lumps.

5. Divide the batter between the prepared tins. Bake for 35–40 minutes, until a skewer inserted into the centre comes out clean. Allow to cool to room temperature before assembling.

6. To make the Cherry Sauce, cut the cherries in half and place in a small pot with the berries, sugar and water. Bring to the boil while stirring, then reduce the heat and simmer for about 10 minutes, until the liquid has reduced and the sauce thickened. Allow to cool to room temperature then chill until needed.

7. To make the Chocolate Ganache, break the chocolate into a microwave-proof bowl, add the cream and microwave for about 1 minute. Whisk until smooth, then let it cool to room temperature and it will thicken.

Continued overleaf . . .

8. To assemble, cut both cakes in half horizontally. Place one layer on a serving plate and drizzle with a third of the Cherry Sauce. Top with a third of the whipped cream and spread out evenly.

9. Repeat with the remaining layers until all the sauce and whipped cream are used up. Spread the Chocolate Ganache over the top of the cake and sprinkle with the grated chocolate.

10. Chill for at least 3 hours or preferably overnight before serving.

Tips and tricks

- *This gateau is even better made a day in advance.*

- *To make things faster you can bake the cakes the day before and store them in an airtight container until needed.*

Peach Galette

Of all the different types of fruit, stone fruit is my absolute favourite.
This beautiful galette really highlights the flavour of the peaches. The
easy home-made pastry tastes like shortbread, but if you want to make it
even easier you can use a block of store-bought sweet short pastry.

Sweet Pastry
1½ cups plain flour
200 g (7 oz) butter, chilled
1 Tbsp sugar
¼ tsp salt

2 Tbsp sugar
2 Tbsp cornflour
½ tsp cinnamon
3–4 peaches, stoned and
  sliced
2 Tbsp lemon juice
1 Tbsp milk
1 tsp sugar, to sprinkle
whipped cream, to serve

1. To make the Sweet Pastry, place the ingredients in a food processor and blitz until a dough ball forms. Wrap in cling film and chill for 20 minutes.

2. Preheat the oven to 180°C (350°F) fan bake. Line a baking tray with baking paper.

3. To prepare the filling, mix the 2 tablespoons of sugar with the cornflour and cinnamon in a large bowl. Add the peach slices and toss to coat. Drizzle the lemon juice over the peaches and mix through.

4. Place the Sweet Pastry in the centre of the prepared tray and roll out to a large circle about 5mm (¼ in) thick. (It doesn't matter if it hangs over the edge of the tray slightly, it will get folded back in.)

5. Arrange the peaches in an even layer on the pastry, leaving a 4 cm (1½ in) border around the outside of the circle. Fold the border back over the peaches, pressing it together slightly as you go.

6. Brush the milk over the pastry then sprinkle with the extra teaspoon of sugar.

7. Bake for 40 minutes, until the pastry is golden and the peaches have cooked through. Serve warm with whipped cream.

Tips and tricks
• *Swap the peaches for plums, apricots, pears or apples if you prefer.*

Happy 40th Laurie Jean

Mini Pavlova Wreath

This extravagant festive wreath has been crazy-popular since I released it on my website in 2020. It's spectacular to look at but actually very easy to put together, because everything can be made in advance and assembled on the day. My huge wooden board is actually made from the lid of a wine barrel!

Mini Pavlovas
4 egg whites
1 tsp white vinegar
1 tsp vanilla essence
1 cup caster sugar

Raspberry Drizzle
1 cup frozen raspberries
1 Tbsp caster sugar

Chocolate Sauce
120 g (4¼ oz) dark chocolate
¾ cup cream

¼ cup passionfruit curd
250 g (9 oz) strawberries
125 g (4½ oz) raspberries
125 g (4½ oz) blueberries
125 g (4½ oz) pomegranate
  seeds
3 kiwifruit, peeled and sliced
flesh of 1 mango, sliced
1 Tbsp icing sugar, to dust
1 handful fresh mint sprigs,
  to serve
30 g (1 oz) Flake bar, to serve
2 cups cream, whipped,
  to serve

1. Preheat the oven to 170°C (325°F) fan bake. Line 2 baking trays with baking paper.

2. To make the Mini Pavlovas, place the egg whites in the bowl of a stand mixer and whisk on high speed until stiff peaks form. Add the vinegar and vanilla then whisk again on a slow speed.

3. Increase the speed to medium and gradually add the sugar. Whisk on high speed for 5 minutes until stiff and glossy.

4. Spoon 10 rounds of meringue onto the prepared trays. Reduce the oven temperature to 120°C (235°F) and bake for 40 minutes, until crisp to the touch.

5. Turn off the oven and allow the pavlovas to cool completely in the oven with the door ajar. Once cool, store in an airtight container in the pantry for up to 4 days.

6. To make the Raspberry Drizzle, combine the raspberries and sugar in a microwave-proof bowl or jug and microwave on high for 1 minute. Stir, microwave for another 20 seconds, then stir again. Set aside to cool, then chill until needed.

7. To make the Chocolate Sauce, break the chocolate into a microwave-proof bowl, add the cream and microwave for 90 seconds. Allow to sit for 2 minutes then stir until smooth. Chill until needed (you may have to warm it slightly before serving).

Continued overleaf . . .

KIDS' FAVE

8. To assemble the wreath, place ramekins of Chocolate Sauce, Raspberry Drizzle and passionfruit curd on a large serving platter. Add the Mini Pavlovas in a circular pattern. Fill in the gaps with the fresh fruit. Sprinkle with the icing sugar and garnish with mint sprigs and crumbled Flake bar. Serve accompanied by bowls of whipped cream.

Tips and tricks

- *The Mini Pavlovas, Chocolate Sauce and Raspberry Drizzle can be made up to 4 days ahead of time and stored in airtight containers until needed.*

- *You can even slice up the mango and kiwifruit in advance, to save you time on Christmas Day.*

- *Feel free to add your favourite fruits. Blackberries, cherries, pineapple, melon and grapes would all work well. Freshly cut limes can add another pop of green.*

Lemon Delicious Pudding

This is one of the first puddings that I posted to my website and my readers and I have loved it ever since. You can make it in one large dish or small individual ramekins. I like to serve it warm with a scoop of vanilla ice cream.

75 g (2½ oz) butter, melted
1 cup milk
3 egg yolks
1 Tbsp finely grated lemon zest
⅓ cup lemon juice
1 cup caster sugar
½ cup self-raising flour
3 egg whites
1 Tbsp icing sugar, to serve

1. Preheat the oven to 170°C (325°F) fan bake. Grease a 27 x 17 cm (10¾ x 6½ in) oven dish.

2. Place the butter, milk, egg yolks, lemon zest and juice in a large bowl and whisk to combine. Sift in the sugar and flour and stir to combine.

3. Place the egg whites in the bowl of a stand mixer and whisk until soft peaks form.

4. Fold half the egg whites into the lemon mixture, then gently fold in the rest.

5. Transfer to the prepared dish. Place the dish in a large roasting tray and pour enough boiling water into the tray to come halfway up the sides of the smaller dish.

6. Bake for 25–30 minutes, until golden and just set.

7. Serve dusted with icing sugar.

Tips and tricks
- *This also works really well with lime juice and zest.*

KIDS' FAVE

Chocolate Whip Cheesecake Cups with Berries

These deconstructed cheesecake cups have it all — a crumbly cookie base, a creamy chocolate cheesecake centre and a tart berry sauce. They can be prepared the day before and topped with fresh berries just before serving.

150 g (5½ oz) plain biscuits
80 g (2¾ oz) butter, melted
2 cups frozen mixed berries
2 Tbsp caster sugar
100 g (3½ oz) milk chocolate
225 g (8 oz) cream cheese, softened
½ cup icing sugar
1 cup cream
sliced fresh strawberries, to serve

Tips and tricks

- *This recipe makes enough for 4 large or 6 small portions.*

- *You can use Super Wine biscuits, Marie biscuits or arrowroot biscuits in this recipe.*

- *Swap the milk chocolate for dark chocolate, Caramilk or white chocolate if you prefer.*

1. To make the cookie crumbs, place the biscuits in a food processor and blitz to a fine crumb. Add the butter and blitz again until combined.

2. To make the berry coulis, combine the berries and sugar in a pot and simmer over a gentle heat until the berries have broken down. Mash any large berries if need be. Set aside to cool, then chill until needed.

3. To make the chocolate whip, break the chocolate into a microwave-proof bowl and microwave in bursts until melted. Allow to cool slightly.

4. Place the cream cheese and icing sugar in the bowl of a stand mixer and whisk until smooth. With the mixer still running, slowly pour in half the cream. Once combined, add the remainder of the cream and continue to whip until soft peaks form.

5. Remove the bowl from the mixer. Gently pour in the cooled melted chocolate, carefully folding it through to create chocolate swirls. Do not combine completely.

6. To assemble, divide half the cookie crumbs between 4–6 glass tumblers. Add half the chocolate whip and then half the berry coulis. Repeat with the remaining cookie crumbs, chocolate whip and berry coulis.

7. Chill for at least 4 hours or overnight, before serving topped with the strawberries.

Layered White Chocolate Mud Cake

The beauty of this cake is that it can be made days in advance and will get fudgier over time. Don't let its simple appearance fool you — it really is something special. I challenge you to stop at one piece!

250 g (9 oz) white chocolate,
  plus extra for garnish
200 g (7 oz) butter, diced
200 ml (7 fl oz) boiling water
1 cup caster sugar
1 tsp vanilla essence
2 eggs, whisked
2 cups plain flour
1 tsp baking powder
1 tsp baking soda
chopped fresh strawberries,
  to serve

White Chocolate Ganache
250 g (9 oz) white chocolate,
  chopped
½ cup cream

1. Preheat the oven to 150°C (300°F) fan bake. Grease the sides of two 17 cm (6½ in) round cake tins and line the bases with baking paper.

2. Break the white chocolate into a large microwave-proof bowl. Add the butter and boiling water, cover and microwave on high for 90 seconds, until almost melted. Allow to sit for a few minutes then gently whisk until smooth.

3. Whisk in the sugar and vanilla. Add the eggs and whisk again. Sift in the flour, baking powder and baking soda and fold together until completely combined.

4. Divide the mixture between the prepared tins. Bake for 50 minutes, until a skewer inserted into the centre comes out clean.

5. Allow to cool in the tins for 10 minutes before transferring to a wire rack to cool completely.

6. To make the White Chocolate Ganache, place the white chocolate and cream in a microwave-proof bowl and microwave for 45 seconds. Allow to sit for 1 minute then whisk until smooth. Chill until it has firmed up and is a good consistency for spreading.

7. To assemble, place one cake on a serving plate and top with half the ganache.

Continued overleaf...

KIDS' FAVE

8. Place the second cake on top and spread with the remaining ganache. Grate extra white chocolate over the top and add the chopped strawberries for decoration.

Tips and tricks

- *This can be made in two small tins, or as one large tray cake. If making as a large cake, increase the cooking time accordingly.*

- *To make ahead of time, wrap the cooled cakes in cling film and store in the fridge for up to 5 days. Add the ganache before serving.*

Stacked Berry Pavlova

An impressive dessert, and an excellent choice when you need to feed a crowd and want to serve up something with the wow factor. The tangy coulis is very quick to make and partners well with the sweet meringue and cream.

4 egg whites
1 cup caster sugar
1 tsp cornflour
1 tsp white vinegar
½ tsp vanilla essence
2 cups cream
1 Tbsp icing sugar
100 g (3½ oz) fresh
 strawberries, sliced
1 handful fresh mint leaves,
 to serve
chocolate curls, to serve

Berry Coulis
500 g (1 lb 2 oz) frozen
 mixed berries
⅓ cup white sugar

1. Preheat the oven to 120°C (235°F). Line 2 baking trays with baking paper.

2. To make the pavlovas, place the egg whites in the bowl of a stand mixer and whisk until stiff. Slowly pour in the sugar and keep beating until very stiff. Add the cornflour, vinegar and vanilla and fold together.

3. Spread in two even rectangles onto the prepared trays. Bake for 1 hour then turn off the oven and allow the pavlovas to cool completely in the oven.

4. To make the Berry Coulis, combine the berries and sugar in a pot and simmer over a gentle heat until the berries have broken down. Mash any large berries if need be. Set aside to cool, then chill until needed.

5. To assemble, place one pavlova on a serving platter. Whip the cream with the icing sugar until soft peaks form.

6. Spread half the whipped cream over the pavlova, then spoon on half the Berry Coulis and spread out to the edges. Finish with the second layer of pavlova and the remaining cream and coulis.

7. Serve topped with the strawberries, mint leaves and chocolate curls.

Tips and tricks

- *It is best to assemble this dessert just before serving.*

- *You can use grated chocolate or a crumbled Flake bar in place of the curls.*

Individual Apple Cobblers

This recipe is so versatile you can use any type of apples, or swap them for your favourite seasonal fruit. You can also make it in one large dish if you prefer.

3 Granny Smith apples
2 Tbsp white sugar
2 Tbsp lemon juice
2 Tbsp water
vanilla ice cream, to serve

Oaty Topping
½ cup rolled oats
½ cup self-raising flour
½ cup white sugar
1 tsp cinnamon
½ cup milk
50 g (1¾ oz) butter, melted

1. Peel and core the apples and cut them into 1 cm (½ in) pieces.

2. Place in a pot with the sugar, lemon juice and water. Simmer gently over a medium heat for 10–15 minutes, stirring occasionally, until the apples soften but still hold their shape. Remove from the heat and set aside.

3. Preheat the oven to 180°C (350°F) fan bake.

4. To make the Oaty Topping, mix the oats, flour, sugar and cinnamon in a bowl. Add the milk and butter and mix to combine.

5. Divide the apple mixture between 4–6 ramekins. Divide the Oaty Topping over the top and spread out evenly.

6. Bake for 35 minutes, until golden and cooked through.

7. Serve warm from the oven with a scoop of ice cream on top of each one.

Brownie Trifle

I have never been a huge fan of traditional trifle, so
I came up with my own recipe using brownie and berries instead.
It is soooo delicious and everyone who makes it loves it!

Brownie
200 g (7 oz) butter, melted
1¾ cup brown sugar
2 eggs
½ cup cocoa powder
1½ cups self-raising flour

300 g (10½ oz) frozen
  raspberries
3 Tbsp caster sugar
250 g (9 oz) fresh
  strawberries, sliced
2 cups cream, whipped
600 g (1lb 5 oz) ready-made
  custard
125 g (4½ oz) fresh
  raspberries, to serve
2 x 30 g (1 oz) Flake bars, to
  serve
1 Tbsp icing sugar, to serve

1. To make the Brownie, preheat the oven to 170°C (325°F)
   fan bake. Line a 27 x 17 cm (10¾ x 6½ in) slice tin with
   baking paper.

2. Whisk together the butter and sugar. Add the eggs and
   cocoa, whisking well after each addition. Sift in the flour and
   fold gently to combine.

3. Transfer to the prepared tin. Bake for 20–25 minutes, until
   cooked through but soft on the outside. Allow to cool, then
   cut into 2.5 cm (1 in) squares, separate into 3 equal piles and
   set aside.

4. To make the raspberry sauce, place the frozen raspberries
   and caster sugar in a microwave-proof bowl or jug and
   microwave on high for 1 minute. Stir, microwave for another
   minute, then stir again. Set aside to cool.

5. To assemble the trifle, arrange half the strawberries in the
   base of a trifle dish or large serving bowl. Top with a third
   of the cooled raspberry sauce, then a third of the brownie
   pieces. Carefully spoon in half the whipped cream.

6. Add a layer of custard and smooth it to the edges with
   a spoon. Add another third of the raspberry sauce, a
   second layer of brownie pieces and then the remaining
   strawberries.

Continued overleaf . . .

KIDS' FAVE

7. Add the remaining custard and smooth to the edges, then top with the remaining brownie pieces and raspberry sauce. Finish with the remaining whipped cream and gently smooth the top.

8. Chill for at least 3 hours before serving.

9. Just before serving, decorate the top with the fresh raspberries, crumbled Flake and a sprinkle of icing sugar.

Tips and tricks

- *This trifle is even better if you make it a day in advance and store it in the fridge overnight.*

Ginger Kisses Cheesecake

Ginger kisses bring up so many childhood memories for me.
To take them into adulthood, I created this creamy cheesecake.
Ginger fans have the option of adding crystallised ginger on top.

250 g (9 oz) packet
  Gingernuts
100 g (3½ oz) butter, melted
2 tsp powdered gelatine
2 tsp cold water
500 g (1 lb 2 oz) cream
  cheese, softened
1 tsp vanilla essence
200 g (7 oz) sour cream
¾ cup caster sugar
200 g (7 oz) packet ginger
  kisses, coarsely chopped
¼ cup chopped crystallised
  ginger (optional)

1. Line the base of a 22 cm (8½ in) round cake tin with baking paper.

2. Place the Gingernuts in a food processor and blitz to a fine crumb. Add the butter and blitz again. Press into the prepared tin and chill while you make the filling.

3. Mix the gelatine and water in a small microwave-proof bowl or jug and set aside.

4. In the bowl of a stand mixer, whip the cream cheese and vanilla until smooth. Add the sour cream and sugar, then mix until the sugar has dissolved.

5. Microwave the gelatine mixture for 15 seconds, until it turns to liquid (it will have thickened up while set aside). Add it to the cream cheese mixture and mix to combine.

6. Add the ginger kisses and fold in evenly.

7. Pour onto the chilled base and decorate with the crystallised ginger (if using).

8. Chill for at least 3 hours or preferably overnight until set.

9. Remove from the tin, slice and serve.

Tips and tricks
• *The base can also be made with plain biscuits.*

Eton Mess Ambrosia

Ambrosia is a classic dessert that generations of Kiwis have enjoyed. In this recipe I've combined ambrosia with another classic dessert, Eton Mess, by using store-bought meringues.

1¼ cups cream
2 cups Greek yoghurt
425 g (15 oz) can boysenberries, drained
200 g (7 oz) marshmallows, halved
3 x 30 g (1 oz) Flake bars
95 g (3¼ oz) packet store-bought meringues, cut into bite-size pieces
500g (1 lb 2 oz) fresh strawberries, finely sliced

1. To make the ambrosia, place the cream in the bowl of a stand mixer and whip until peaks form.

2. Add the yoghurt, boysenberries and marshmallows. Crumble in one of the Flake bars and mix until well combined.

3. To assemble, layer the ambrosia, meringue pieces, strawberries and second crumbled Flake bar into 6–8 glass tumblers.

4. Chill for at least 3 hours before serving with the remaining Flake bar crumbled on top.

Tips and tricks

- *I like to cut the meringues instead of crushing them. This keeps the pretty swirls intact and makes the dessert look even more impressive.*

- *Feel free to use your favourite combination of fruit and berries.*

KIDS' FAVE

Baked Lemon and Passionfruit Cheesecake

I'm a big fan of baked cheesecakes, but many people find the thought of making them intimidating, so I've broken down the recipe for this creamy New York-style cheesecake into simple steps.

250 g (9 oz) packet malt biscuits
120 g (4¼ oz) butter, melted
450 g (1 lb) cream cheese, at room temperature
1 cup caster sugar
¾ cup cream
finely grated zest of 1 lemon
juice of 1 lemon
4 eggs
flesh of 1 ripe mango, thinly sliced
¼ cup passionfruit syrup

1. Preheat the oven to 150°C (300°F) fan bake. Line the base of a 22 cm (8½ in) round cake tin with baking paper.

2. To make the base, place the biscuits in a food processor and blitz to a fine crumb. Add the butter and blitz again. Press into the prepared tin and chill while you make the filling.

3. Place the cream cheese and sugar in the bowl of a stand mixer and beat until well combined. Add the cream, lemon zest and juice and mix again.

4. Add the eggs one at a time, mixing between each addition. Scrape down the sides of the bowl and mix one last time on high speed until well combined.

5. Place the cake tin on a baking tray to catch any leaks while baking. Pour the cream cheese mixture over the biscuit base.

6. Bake for 70 minutes. At this point the cheesecake should still wobble in the centre. Turn off the oven and allow the cheesecake to cool in the oven with the door ajar. Chill until cold and set or overnight.

7. Just before serving, arrange the mango strips on the cheesecake and top with the passionfruit syrup.

Tips and tricks
- *If you can't get your hands on fresh mango you can use canned mango or fresh berries instead.*

Acknowledgements

Firstly, I'd like to say thanks to you for buying this book and supporting me to become a cookbook author. Five years ago I would never have dreamed this could happen. Also, thank you to all my followers on Facebook, Instagram and TikTok for encouraging me to create a second book.

I want to thank my family: Mikey, Archie and Henry. We have an awesome life together. Thank you for being my taste testers, offering your honest opinions and championing everything I do.

A huge thanks to my big, extended family! I'm so lucky to have you all. I love doing life with you.

Thanks to Michelle, Leanne and the team at Allen & Unwin for doing such a super job with *Everyday Favourites* that everyone loved it and now we are on to the second one! You have been awesome and so great to work with.

And to the 'dream team': photographer Mel Jenkins and food stylist Jo Bridgford. I had so much fun shooting the recipes with you in the studio. You are both so talented and you really brought my food to life. While cooking 10 recipes a day was full-on, you made it easy for me, and the result speaks for itself in this incredible cookbook.

Another big thank you to Lottie Hedley.

Terrible weather meant that our cover and lifestyle shoot got postponed a few times, but luckily we ended up with a beautiful day, taking photos at our home and out on the lake in Taupō. It was such a pleasure to take you on our boat and show you all the favourite places we go to as a family.

Thanks to my VJ Cooks team: Theresa, Erin S, Erin H, Grace and Holly. You guys are the best and we have so much fun working together. I love the team we are building. You all rock!

Thanks to Jane Binsley for editing the recipes. And thanks to Kate for designing the book. I loved the first one and this one is just as amazing!

Lastly, to all my wonderful friends who have supported me every step of the way and who went straight out to buy the first book: thank you for coming with me on this journey. I couldn't have done it without you.

Vanya x

Image Credits

Melanie Jenkins (Flash Studios) back cover, pages 14–27, 31–59, 63–77, 81–89, 92–103, 107–135, 139–179, 183–187, 191–195

Lottie Hedley front cover and flaps, pages 2–13, 28–29, 60–61, 78–79, 91, 104, 105, 136, 137, 181, 189, 196–208

Index

A

aioli, lemon 42
almond and apricot rocky road 144
almond and cranberry bliss balls 156
ambrosia, Eton mess 192
apple cobblers, individual 184
Apricot and Almond Rocky Road 144
Apricot and Lemon Bliss Balls 156
Asian Slaw with Crispy Noodles 112
Avocado, Corn, Tomato and Black Bean Salad 114

B

Baked Lemon and Passionfruit Cheesecake 194
balls, bliss 156
banana cake, chocolate 124
Barbecued Fish Tacos with Pineapple Salsa 18
Barbecued Lamb Kofta Platter 32
Barbecued Lamb Steaks with Home-made Chimichurri 40
Barbecued Satay Chicken Skewers 22
Barbecued Steak Fajitas 58
Barbecued Zucchini Salad with Feta Whip 108
bars, nut and seed 148
batter, beer 52
beef
  Barbecued Steak Fajitas 58
  Beef and Noodle Stir-fry 84
  Korean Beef on Rice 74

Meatball Subs 64
One-pot Meatballs and Gnocchi 48
Thai Beef Salad 96
Beef and Noodle Stir-fry 84
beef salad, Thai 96
Beer Batter 52
Beer-battered Fish Burgers 52
berries
  Black Forest Gateau 164
  Brownie Trifle 186
  Chocolate Whip Cheesecake Cups with Berries 176
  Eton Mess Ambrosia 192
  Mini Pavlova Wreath 170
  Stacked Berry Pavlova 182
berry pavlova, stacked 182
black bean, corn, avocado and tomato salad 114
Black Forest Gateau 164
Bliss Balls Four Ways 156
blueberry and lemon loaf 126
bread see pizza and bread
Breakfast Pizza Slab 30
brie and cranberry wreath 34
broccoli salad, raw 106
brownie slice, marshmallow 132
Brownie Trifle 186
brownies, red velvet 154
burgers, beer-battered fish 52

C

Caesar Dressing 102
Caesar salad, chicken 102
cakes and loaves
  Black Forest Gateau 164
  Chocolate Banana Cake 124
  Date Loaf 134
  Layered White Chocolate Mud Cake 178

Lemon and Blueberry Loaf 126
Upside-down Plum Cake 142
Caramel Filling (Crispy Cashew Slice) 122
caramel slice, crispy cashew 122
Caramilk Rocky Road 144
cashew caramel slice, crispy 122
cauliflower, pumpkin and haloumi curry 82
cheese scones, the easiest 130
cheesecake cups, chocolate whip, with berries 176
cheesecakes
  Baked Lemon and Passionfruit Cheesecake 194
  Chocolate Whip Cheesecake Cups with Berries 176
  Ginger Kisses Cheesecake 190
chicken
  Barbecued Satay Chicken Skewers 22
  Chicken and Zucchini Pesto Pasta 38
  Chicken Caesar Salad 102
  Chicken Parmigiana Tray Bake 76
  Chicken, Corn and Spinach Filo Pie 50
  Classic Chicken Korma 56
  Crispy Coating (for chicken) 68
  Herby Chicken Dippers 36
  Mexican Chicken Salad 98
  One-pot Chicken and Lemon Orzo 88
  Southern-style Fried Chicken 68
  Sticky Pineapple Chicken Bowls 54
chicken and lemon orzo, one-pot 88

Chicken and Zucchini Pesto Pasta 38
chicken bowls, sticky pineapple 54
Chicken Caesar Salad 102
chicken dippers, herby 36
Chicken Parmigiana Tray Bake 76
chicken salad, Mexican 98
chicken skewers, barbecued satay 22
Chicken, Corn and Spinach Filo Pie 50
Chimichurri 40
Chipotle Dressing 98
Chipotle Mayo 58
chipotle sauce, herby 24
chocolate
  Apricot and Almond Rocky Road 144
  Black Forest Gateau 164
  Brownie Trifle 186
  Caramilk Rocky Road 144
  Chocolate Banana Cake 124
  Chocolate Fish Slice 138
  Chocolate Icing 124
  Chocolate Layer (Crispy Cashew Slice) 122
  Chocolate Muffins 146
  Chocolate Rice Bubble Slice 150
  Chocolate Topping 138
  Chocolate Whip Cheesecake Cups with Berries 176
  Layered White Chocolate Mud Cake 178
  Marshmallow Brownie Slice 132
  Red Velvet Brownies 154
  Rocky Road Four Ways 144
  Triple Chocolate Cookies 152
  Turkish Delight Rocky Road 144
  Weet-Bix and Dark Chocolate

Bliss Balls 156
  White Chocolate and Cranberry Rocky Road 144
Chocolate Banana Cake 124
chocolate cookies, triple 152
Chocolate Fish Slice 138
Chocolate Icing 124
Chocolate Layer (Crispy Cashew Slice) 122
chocolate mud cake, white, layered 178
Chocolate Muffins 146
Chocolate Rice Bubble Slice 150
Chocolate Topping 138
Chocolate Whip Cheesecake Cups with Berries 176
Classic Chicken Korma 56
coating, crispy 68
cob loaf, creamy spinach 26
cobblers, individual apple 184
cocktail salad, prawn 110
cookies, triple chocolate 152
corn, avocado, tomato and black bean salad 114
corn, chicken and spinach filo pie 50
couscous, roasted vegetable salad 100
Cranberry and Almond Bliss Balls 156
cranberry and brie wreath 34
cranberry and white chocolate rocky road 144
Creamy Pesto Dressing 100
Creamy Spinach Cob Loaf 26
Crispy Cashew Caramel Slice 122
Crispy Coating (for chicken) 68
Crispy Tuna Cakes 42
crunch, ginger slice
curries
  Classic Chicken Korma 56
  Pumpkin, Haloumi and Cauliflower Curry 82

curry, pumpkin, haloumi and cauliflower 82

D
dark chocolate and Weet-Bix bliss balls 156
date and peanut butter bliss balls 156
Date Loaf 134
dippers, herby chicken 36
dipping sauce, minty 26
dough, pizza 30
dressings and mayos
  Caesar Dressing 102
  Chipotle Dressing 98
  Chipotle Mayo 58
  Creamy Pesto Dressing 100
  Lime Dressing 114
  Marie Rose Dressing 110
  Miso Dressing 112
  Pesto Dressing 116
  Thai Dressing 96

E
Eton Mess Ambrosia 192

F
fajitas, barbecued steak 58
feta
  Barbecued Lamb Kofta Platter 32
  Barbecued Zucchini Salad with Feta Whip 108
  Roasted Pumpkin and Feta Tart 20
  Roasted Vegetable Couscous Salad 100
feta and roasted pumpkin tart 20
Feta Whip 108
filling, caramel 122
fillings, toppings and icings
  Caramel Filling (Crispy Cashew Slice) 122

Chocolate Icing 124
Chocolate Layer (Crispy
Cashew Slice) 122
Chocolate Topping 138
Ginger Icing 140
Lemon Glaze 126
Marshmallow Topping 132
Plum Topping 142
filo pie, chicken, corn and
spinach 50
fish
Barbecued Fish Tacos with
Pineapple Salsa 18
Beer-battered Fish Burgers 52
Crispy Tuna Cakes 42
Quick Smoked Salmon Pasta
with Capers 62
Salmon and Warm Potato Salad
116
fish burgers, beer-battered 52
fish tacos, barbecued with
pineapple salsa 18
fried chicken, Southern-style 68

G

galette, peach 168
gateau, Black Forest 164
Ginger Crunch Slice 140
Ginger Icing 140
Ginger Kisses Cheesecake 190
glaze, lemon 126
gnocchi and meatballs, one-pot
48

H

haloumi, pumpkin and
cauliflower curry 82
Herby Chicken Dippers 36
Herby Chipotle Sauce 24

I

icing see fillings, toppings and
icings

icing, chocolate 124
Individual Apple Cobblers 184

K

kofta platter, barbecued lamb
32
Korean Beef on Rice 74
korma, classic chicken 56

L

lamb
Barbecued Lamb Kofta Platter
32
Barbecued Lamb Steaks with
Home-made Chimichurri 40
Moroccan Lamb Pies 86
One-pot Meatballs and
Gnocchi 48
lamb pies, Moroccan 86
lamb steaks, barbecued with
home-made chimichurri 40
lamb, barbecued kofta platter
32
lasagne, vegetarian 70
Layered White Chocolate Mud
Cake 178
Lemon Aioli 42
lemon and apricot bliss balls 156
Lemon and Blueberry Loaf 126
lemon and chicken orzo, one-pot
88
lemon and passionfruit
cheesecake, baked 194
Lemon Delicious Pudding 174
Lemon Glaze 126
lettuce cups, pork 80
Lime Dressing 114
loaves see cakes and loaves
Lolly Slice 128

M

Marie Rose Dressing 110
marinade, satay 22

Marshmallow Brownie Slice 132
Marshmallow Topping 132
mayo, chipotle 58
mayos see dressings and mayos
Meatball Subs 64
meatballs and gnocchi, one-pot
48
meringue
Eton Mess Ambrosia 192
Mini Pavlova Wreath 170
Passionfruit Meringue Pie 162
Stacked Berry Pavlova 182
meringue pie, passionfruit 162
Mexican Chicken Salad 98
Mini Pavlova Wreath 170
Minty Dipping Sauce 26
Miso Dressing 112
Moroccan Lamb Pies 86
mud cake, white chocolate,
layered 178
muffins, chocolate 146

N

noodles
Asian Slaw with Crispy Noodles
112
Beef and Noodle Stir-fry 84
nut and seed bars 148

O

One-pot Chicken and Lemon
Orzo 88
One-pot Meatballs and Gnocchi
48
orzo, chicken and lemon orzo
88

P

passionfruit and lemon
cheesecake, baked 194
Passionfruit Meringue Pie 162
pasta
Chicken and Zucchini Pesto
Pasta 38

One-pot Chicken and Lemon Orzo 88
One-pot Meatballs and Gnocchi 48
Quick Smoked Salmon Pasta with Capers 62
Vegetarian Lasagne 70
pavlova wreath, mini 170
pavlova, stacked berry 182
Peach Galette 168
Peanut Butter and Date Bliss Balls 156
peanuts
  Barbecued Satay Chicken Skewers 22
  Peanut Butter and Date Bliss Balls 156
  Pork Lettuce Cups 80
  Satay Marinade 22
  Thai Beef Salad 96
Pesto Dressing 116
pesto dressing, creamy 100
pesto, chicken and zucchini pasta 38
pie, chicken, corn and spinach filo pie 50
pies and tarts
  Chicken, Corn and Spinach Filo Pie 50
  Moroccan Lamb Pies 86
  Peach Galette 168
  Roasted Pumpkin and Feta Tart 20
pineapple chicken bowls, sticky 54
Pineapple Salsa 18
pizza and bread
  Breakfast Pizza Slab 30
  Creamy Spinach Cob Loaf 26
  Pizza Dough 30
  XL Brie and Cranberry Wreath 34
Pizza Dough 30
pizza slab, breakfast 30

plum cake, upside-down 142
Plum Topping 142
pork
  One-pot Meatballs and Gnocchi 48
  Pork Lettuce Cups 80
  Sweet and Sour Pork 66
Pork Lettuce Cups 80
pork, sweet and sour 66
potato salad, warm with salmon 116
potatoes, smashed with herby chipotle sauce 24
Prawn Cocktail Salad 110
pudding, lemon delicious 174
pumpkin and feta tart 20
Pumpkin, Haloumi and Cauliflower Curry 82

Q
Quick Smoked Salmon Pasta with Capers 62

R
Raw Broccoli Salad 106
Red Velvet Brownies 154
rice and rice bowls
  Korean Beef on Rice 74
  Sticky Pineapple Chicken Bowls 54
rice bubble slice, chocolate 150
Roasted Pumpkin and Feta Tart 20
Roasted Vegetable Couscous Salad 100
Rocky Road Four Ways 144

S
salads
  Asian Slaw with Crispy Noodles 112
  Avocado, Corn, Tomato and Black Bean Salad 114

Barbecued Zucchini Salad with Feta Whip 108
Chicken Caesar Salad 102
Mexican Chicken Salad 98
Prawn Cocktail Salad 110
Raw Broccoli Salad 106
Roasted Vegetable Couscous Salad 100
Salmon and Warm Potato Salad 116
Thai Beef Salad 96
Salmon and Warm Potato Salad 116
salmon pasta with capers, quick 62
salsa, pineapple 18
satay chicken skewers, barbecued 22
Satay Marinade 22
sauces and salsas
  Chimichurri 40
  Chipotle Mayo 58
  Feta Whip 108
  Herby Chipotle Sauce 24
  Lemon Aioli 42
  Minty Dipping Sauce 26
  Pineapple Salsa 18
  Stir-fry Sauce 84
  Sweet and Sour Sauce 66
  White Sauce 70
scones, the easiest cheese 130
Seed and Nut Bars 148
skewers, barbecued chicken satay 22
slaw, Asian with crispy noodles 112
slices
  Chocolate Fish Slice 138
  Chocolate Rice Bubble Slice 150
  Crispy Cashew Caramel Slice 122
  Ginger Crunch Slice 140
  Lolly Slice 128